D1598190

Walt Disney World for Teens and Tweens

Tim Brooks

Theme Park Press
www.ThemeParkPress.com

© 2016 Tim Brooks

No part of this publication may be reproduced, distributed, or transmitted in any form or by any means, including photocopying, recording, or other electronic or mechanical methods, without the prior written permission of the publisher, except for brief quotations embodied in critical reviews and certain other noncommercial uses permitted by copyright law.

Although every precaution has been taken to verify the accuracy of the information contained herein, no responsibility is assumed for any errors or omissions, and no liability is assumed for damages that may result from the use of this information.

Theme Park Press is not associated with the Walt Disney Company.

The views expressed in this book are those of the author and do not necessarily reflect the views of Theme Park Press.

Theme Park Press publishes its books in a variety of print and electronic formats. Some content that appears in one format may not appear in another.

Editor: Bob McLain
Layout: Artisanal Text

ISBN 978-1-941500-97-2
Printed in the United States of America

Theme Park Press | www.ThemeParkPress.com
Address queries to bob@themeparkpress.com

Contents

Introduction

For Tweens

Walt Disney World is one of the most magical places on earth and is filled with fun and adventure for people of all ages. In this book I will take you through the exciting attractions, wide variety of restaurants, and wonderfully themed resorts that Disney World has to offer.

This book can be used to help you work with your parents in planning a vacation that everyone can enjoy. You will notice that every attraction has some time of "educational slant". A lot of families go on vacation at Disney World while school is in session. These "educational slants" can be presented to your teachers to help develop special projects for you work on while on your vacation. I know, it does not sound like fun, but, trust me, you will be having more fun than your classmates who are stuck in school.

For Adults

This book is designed for your children to use in conjunction with any Disney World guidebook that you may also purchase to help plan your Disney World vacation. When you are planning your vacation, bring the kids and have them grab this book and work alongside them. The more the kids feel included, they will gain some ownership in the vacation which should lead to a more enjoyable experience.

There is an "educational slant" section for every attraction. These are ideas that you can present to your children's teachers for projects that they can work on at Disney World. Some schools and teachers are supportive of a Disney World vacation and will not put up much resistance for pulling the kids out of school. However, there are some schools and teachers who are not as supportive. These "educational slants" can help you be more pro-active in showing that a Disney World vacation can be a learning experience (and one not just limited to the different cultures of Epcot's World Showcase).

Planning for Your Vacation

A Disney World vacation is something that cannot be planned overnight. Planning a Disney World vacation is a lot of work. It is work that I enjoy. This book, in addition to helping you plan your vacation, will also inform you about key dates leading up to it. These dates are important because they will help you and your family obtain the dining reservations and FastPass+ times that you want and not be stuck with what's left over.

There are three big dates in planning your vacation: 365 days before, 180 days before, and 60 days before.

365 Days Before Your Vacation

This is the first day you can book a full package (room, park tickets, and a Disney dining plan). You will have the widest selection of resorts available. Park tickets and dining plans are always available. But booking the reservation as a package is easier than booking a room and then adding tickets and dining plans later in the process. You only need to put down a $200 deposit, with the balance due 45 days before your vacation begins.

Once your vacation is booked, your package rates (room, ticket, and dining) are locked in. They cannot increase even if Disney raises prices between when you booked your vacation and when your vacation begins. This is the most important benefit to planning vacation early. It allows your parents to lock in a rate and start saving with the goal of having the vacation paid off by the 45-day deadline.

Should a special discount or promotion come out during this time, you MAY be eligible to apply that discount or promotion to your existing reservation. But I tell everyone to plan and budget for what you can afford; consider any discounts or promotions that can be applied to your vacation as a bonus. Never plan your budget around getting a discount or a promotion—it may only lead to disappointment.

180 Days Before Your Vacation

You can now make all of your Disney dining reservations, in either of two ways: on the Disney World website starting at 6 a.m. Eastern or by calling 407-WDW-DINE starting at 7 a.m. Eastern. Have multiple electronic devices when attempting to make reservations through the website. The Disney World web servers are not the most stable and are prone to crashing or not working on a specific web browser. When my family makes our dining reservations, we have multiple devices—laptop, tablet, and desktop—at the ready in case of a problem. Calling in means waiting in a phone line as people who are using the web-based reservation system are potentially making reservations in front of you.

Another little tip is to plan the "hard to get reservations" for the end of your trip as opposed to the beginning. At the beginning of your vacation, you are competing against the people are already on vacation in addition to the people whose vacation is starting. At the end of your vacation, you are competing mostly against the people whose vacation started around the same time as yours did.

60 Days Before Your Vacation

This is the last major planning date. You can now make your FastPass+ reservations. These reservations can be made starting at midnight Eastern time. Each guest gets three FastPass+ reservations for EACH day of their Disney World vacation. A FastPass+ reservation allows you to bypass the traditional stand-by line for the FastPass+ line which is, on average, a quarter of the wait time of the posted stand-by time. So, if the stand-by line is 60 minutes, the FastPass+ line, on average, will be around 15 minutes. A reservation is good for one hour and once that hour passes, the FastPass+ reservation is no longer valid and will not be accepted by the FastPass+ reservation system.

Magic Kingdom and Animal Kingdom have a simple system for making reservations. Every attraction that is available for FastPass+ reservations can be selected. However, Epcot and Hollywood Studios have tiered systems for the FastPass+ reservations. You must choose from attractions in Tier 1 and Tier 2 when making their reservations.

Epcot
Tier 1 (choose one)

- Eat to the Beat Concert Series (seasonal)
- Preferred Seating for Illuminations
- Living with the Land
- Mission: SPACE
- Soarin'
- Test Track

Tier 2 (choose two)

- Epcot Character Spot
- Journey Into Imagination with Figment
- Spaceship Earth
- The Seas with Nemo and Friends
- Turtle Talk with Crush

Hollywood Studios

Tier 1 (choose one)

- Beauty and the Beast—Live on Stage
- Preferred Viewing Area for Fantasmic!
- Rock 'n' Roller Coaster
- The Great Movie Ride
- Toy Story Midway Mania

Tier 2 (choose two)

- Disney Junior—Live on Stage
- For the First Time in Forever: A "Frozen" Sing-Along Celebration
- Preferred Seating for Indiana Jones Epic Stunt Spectacular!
- Muppetvision 3D
- Star Tours
- Tower of Terror
- Voyage of the Little Mermaid

After you use your three FastPass+ reservations for the day, you can make a fourth FastPass+ reservation, and once you use the fourth reservation, you can make a fifth, and so on. Because of this, FastPass+ reservations are most difficult to obtain early in the day because people want to make their reservations early so they can be used quickly and then new ones can be obtained. A word of warning about making reservations for preferred seating at nighttime shows and fireworks: these events take place late at night and close to park close which will leave you little time to use any extra FastPass+ reservations for those days. If you are fine with only using three reservations for that day, of course, it's fine.

If you did not get that FastPass+ reservation that you really wanted, do not give up hope. These reservations change all the time, especially closer to your vacation and during your vacation as people shuffle their reservations around to better suit their day in the parks. So, check the system often. There are a lot of people in the parks even on the slowest days, so there is a lot of potential for FastPass+ reservations to change.

Getting There: Entertainment

There are three ways to get from your house to Walt Disney World: by plane, by train, or by car. Each involve some amount from travel to get from Point A to Point B, and let's face it: travel is boring. There is only so much scenery that you can look out at from the car or train window and blue sky is blue sky whether the plane is over your house or over Florida. So, let's take a brief look at some ways that you can entertain yourself during the many hours of travel.

Download some movies to your iPad or use the Disney Movies Anywhere app to view movies already downloaded to your tablet device. A movie will take up a good 90 to 120 minutes which should cover most plane flights, especially now that airlines allow small electronic devices (like tablets) to be used during takeoff and landing. If you have a longer flight, download a couple of movies. A word of warning about the Disney Movies Anywhere app: it needs a strong wireless signal to start the movie even if that movie is already downloaded to your device. I ran into this problem with my daughter's iPad on a recent trip to Disneyland. We had movies downloaded through the app, but because the plane's wireless signal wasn't strong enough, the movies would not start and led to a very upset tween who slept for some of the flight but was bored while awake.

The next easiest thing to do is to bring some books along on the trip. It's easy to get lost in a book and the next thing you know you have arrived in Orlando.

A great thing to do, especially on the way down to Disney World, is any homework assigned by your teachers.

There are not a lot of distractions and you can concentrate on getting your homework done. The sooner it's done, the less time you have to spend on doing it during your vacation or, even worse, rushing to get it done on the trip back home. Think about it: would you rather be enjoying your vacation or worrying about when your homework is going to get done.

Getting There: Planning

Figuring out how to get to Disney World is a great lesson in planning and budgeting that parents can share with their children. Like I mentioned earlier, there are three main ways to get to Disney World: plane, train, and automobile.

Most people will arriving by plane. It is important to know that there are two airports in the Orlando area: Orlando International Airport (MCO), where the majority of flights land and where Disney operates their Magical Express service to and from the airport, and Sanford Airport (SFB), where some minor airlines offer flights to and from select cities. Disney does not operate their Magical Express service from this airport. You are left on your own to find transportation to and from the airport.

Parents, when searching for flights, bring the kids into the process. Show them that there are individual airline websites as well as websites where you can compare the different airlines side by side. Also, take the time to research nearby airports. In searching for flights to Orlando, sometimes the closest airport is not necessarily the most affordable one. So, it can pay to do some searching, even if the result means taking a short drive to a more affordable airport.

If you take the AutoTrain from Lorton, VA, you'll depart at 4 p.m. and arrive in Sanford, FL, the next day, at 4 p.m. This is a great option for people who live a good distance from Disney and don't want to drive the entire way, but still want the freedom of having a car when they are at Disney

World. It can be expensive, though. If you reserve a state-room, it can be as expensive as flying, but you have your own private space which comes in handy during the overnight hours. Amtrak also makes stops in Orlando and Kissimmee, for those who don't want to bring along their car.

The last option is driving. Parents, get the children involved in planning the route that the family is going to take and, if necessary, research hotels where you are going to stop for the night. Before the trip, plan out how much the tolls, if any, are going to be, and when traveling get receipts for the gas and hotels. When you get home, the family can see how much money they saved by driving instead of flying. Budgeting is an important skill for kids to develop, and a vacation is a great example of showing them how important it can be.

CHAPTER ONE

Disney Magic

Before Your Vacation

The Walt Disney World magic starts the moment you and your parents book your Disney World vacation and the family has set up their My Disney Experience account on the Disney World website. One of the first things that you and your family will be able to do is customize your MagicBands. These MagicBands are your "Key to the World" during your Disney World Vacation. The MagicBands are worn around your wrist much like a watch and are used as your room key and park ticket; they can also be used for any charges back to the room (parents: you will have the ability to restrict the charging privileges of your children's cards). These bands are available in a variety of colors and you can customize the name on the band. Solid color MagicBands are free as part of your Disney World vacation package. You can customize bands with Disney characters and attraction themes for an additional fee through the on-line Disney store.

The magic continues as you get closer and closer to your vacation. One of the first packages that will arrive is the one that includes all of the things that are included in your vacation. In the past, this has included a magnet featuring Dumbo which has important dates to remember before your vacation. As you get closer to your vacation, you will receive your Disney's Magical Express package in the mail. Magical Express is one of the best features of a Disney World vacation. Guests flying in and out of Orlando International Airport have ability to take Magical Express. This free service provides shuttle bus transportation from the airport directly to your resort. This is a great service especially if you plan to stay on Disney property for your entire vacation. At the end of your vacation, Magical Express will take you and your family back to Orlando International Airport. Your travel party will be assigned a departure time usually three hours before your flight's scheduled departure.

Included in your Disney's Magical Express package are very important yellow airport-style luggage tags. These tags have your name and resort printed on them. It is important to put these tags on any checked bags before you check-in. These tags allow you to go straight from your plane to the Magical Express check-in area to board your bus to the resort. Disney will grab your bags (for arrivals before 10 p.m.) and deliver them straight to your resort room. Your bags will, in most cases, arrive at the resort three to four hours AFTER you arrive. When flying, I always pack a day's worth of clothes and my swimsuit in a carry-on bag so I have a change of clothes if something delays Magical Express.

The final package will contain your MagicBands. This package arrives around five weeks before your vacation is scheduled to begin. It includes all of your travel party's MagicBands displayed neatly like little wrist watches with each guest's band nickname underneath. These bands come pre-loaded with all of your travel information (pre-purchased tickets, Magical Express—in case those documents are forgotten at home—and dining/room charging privileges). Your bands will be encoded with your room information upon check-in at the resort.

At the Resort

The Disney World resorts are filled with things for both kids and parents to see and explore. It could be the Lion King play area or a giant Mickey Mouse on a swing outside the Contemporary or posing for a picture with the Three Caballros outside Coronado Springs.

Your hotel room will have plenty of theming as well. Look at everything in the room; there is Disney magic hidden everywhere. Some are easy to see like the pictures of the princesses and princes in a Royal Room at Port Orleans Riverside or the Pongo outside All-Star Movies. Others are hidden. It could be a set of Mickey Mouse ears inside the comforter at the Contemporary or possibly Tic-Toc Croc will be watching over your children as they sleep in one of the day-style beds in a room at Port Orleans French Quarter.

Parents, if there is a long wait at the check-in counter, don't worry. There is plenty for the kids to see and do in the lobbies of these resorts as well. Most resorts have classic Mickey Mouse cartoons or current Disney Channel programming playing on one of the televisions near the check-in desk. This is in addition to such things as the giant vintage globe at the center of the Yacht Club lobby or the "hot springs" inside the Wilderness Lodge resort. No matter where you go at Disney World, the magic is everywhere.

In the Parks

Disney magic is in great abundance inside the parks of Disney World. Everywhere you look in the parks, you will come across some Disney magic. For example, on Main Street, U.S.A. at Magic Kingdom, Disney Imagineers pay tribute to the Disney legends who came before them by putting their names in the windows above the store fronts. Look on the ground while walking in the parks; Disney Imagineering even happens here. Guests visiting

Future World at night, for example, can walk through fields of blinking stars near Spaceship Earth. In the new section of Fantasyland, Imagineers did some of their best work. Look on the ground near Dumbo and see how many peanuts you can find embedded in the concrete. Guests with peanut allergies do not worry—these are not actual peanuts. Near Journey of the Little Mermaid, you will find seashells and other whosits and whatsits galore in the pavement.

The best things to look for, and one of the many games that you can play while waiting in line for the attractions, is to look for hidden Mickey shapes. Some of these Hidden Mickeys are put there intentionally by Disney Imagineers while others could just be the way pebbles, rocks, water droplets, etc. have formed during the day. When in line for an attraction, compete against yourself or your siblings or your parents for how many Hidden Mickeys you can find during your wait for the attraction.

These Hidden Mickeys are not just found in the line for attractions. They can be found everywhere and anywhere on Disney World property. They can be found in the restaurants, the décor of the resorts, the interior of your resort room, and even on Disney transportation.

Disney's cast members will get in on the magic as well. Some cast members have been trained or have learned from other cast members how to draw Disney characters using just water. Other cast members will draw hopscotch boards using chalk. One time, in the United Kingdom, my family was able to watch a cast member draw a hopscotch board in the design of Manchester United soccer jerseys. Another time we were in a line to meet Phineas and Ferb at Hollywood Studios. The line for this meet and greet was not well defined, so the cast member took out some chalk and make a make-shift stop sign using Ferb's head to make the "p" in stop. Little things that don't seem like a lot on the surface can go a long way in extending the Disney magic throughout your day in the park.

Another way to have Disney magic in the parks and won't cost a lot (in the beginning) is to get involved in pin trading. Many of the Disney shops sell entry level pin trading kits. These kits, typically, consist of a lanyard and about six to eight pins. Now you can start trading your pins for those of other pin traders and cast members who wear specially colored pin lanyards. Pin trading is a great low-cost souvenir even if you don't trade the pins with anyone else. But be warned, pin trading can be addicting and cost a lot of money if you buy more and more to add to you collection. A $8 or $10 pin does not sound like much when dealing with just one pin. However, when you start talking about a large number of pins, you can easily spend hundreds if not thousands of dollars on a pin collection. Pin collecting is fun and has a low cost entry point, but can get very expensive if you are not careful.

Handling Long Attraction Wait Times

Trying to finding Hidden Mickeys is just one of many ways that you can pass the time while waiting to go on an attraction or see a show. Batteries for phones and tablets will only last so long if you try to use them every time that you are stuck in a long wait for an attraction. Some of the lines are indoors, so it may difficult to get a wireless or cellular signal to your device which will only drain the battery even more. If you don't bring headphones, the sound will be kept down all the way so your device is not distracting to other guests or to the cast members who may be performing a pre-show before some attractions.

Disney Imagineering is making an effort to design queues which are more interactive for guests and one attraction—Dumbo—even has a play area for kids while they wait for their turn to soar through the sky with Dumbo and Timothy Mouse. Some attractions, like Space

Mountain, now have games that guests can play while they make their way through the queue. Other attractions, like The Many Adventures of Winnie the Pooh, allow you to explore The Hundred Acre Wood, which includes a "honey wall", with Winnie the Pooh and his friends.

Kids of all ages will sometimes bond and talk to the kids around them in the queue. They are "stuck" in the same situation and this is a great way to learn about other parts of the United States and the world. Who knows, maybe the kids will make a new friend or maybe even a new pen pal just through waiting in a line at a Disney World attraction.

Disney Meet and Greets

Back in the early days of Disney World, characters used to just roam around the parks meeting guests. Now, the demand to meet these characters is so high that it is rare to meet a character that is just roaming around the park. Meeting has become more formalized. There are three primary ways to meet your favorite Disney character.

- Formal. This type of meet and greet is listed on the park map as an attraction, for example, meeting Mickey and Minnie at the Town Square Plaza on Main Street, U.S.A.

- Informal. This type of meet and greet only runs during certain times of the day and/or the location may have a "rotation" of characters that is going through. For example, as you enter Future World in Epcot, there are a few characters who are available for meet and greets. These characters are usually Daisy Duck, Pluto, and Goofy, but all of the characters may not be present for the entire time. So, you may be in line to meet Daisy, but by the time you reach the front of the line, you may be meeting Goofy instead. Another version is an outside meet and greet with a character, but the character is available for a period of time in the morning and early afternoon. Then the character takes a long break before reappearing in the early evening. Some examples: Snow White meets guests in the German Pavilion of the World Showcase and Mary Poppins meets guests in the United Kingdom, but they only meet from 11 a.m. to 2 p.m. and then from 5 p.m. to 8 p.m. For most accurate information about this type of character meet and greet, consult the My Disney Experience app on your phone or tablet.

- A character palooza. This is the least formal type of meet and greet. It is usually unannounced (though Hollywood Studios, in the past, had a more formalized palooza) and involves a number of characters coming out and meeting guests. These meet and greets are a great way to meet some of the "rarer" Disney characters, like Max Goof, Goofy's son; Baloo from *The Jungle Book*, and Tweedle-dee and Tweedle-dum from *Alice in Wonderland*.

Souvenir Budgeting and Buying

Souvenir budgeting and buying is one of the most difficult parts of a Disney World vacation. This is one place where, if you and your parents do not set strict budgets or restriction on the MagicBands, you can really overspend. Souvenirs and opportunities to purchase souvenirs are everywhere. From the moment you get off the plane in Orlando to the moment you go back through security in Orlando for your flight home, there are opportunities to purchase souvenirs. Souvenirs can be as simple as a postcard or a Mickey-shaped magnet and can be eas laborate and expensive as a $10,000 diamond encrusted statue of Cinderella Castle. Kids: this is where you need to work with your parents about how much money you can bring and how much you can spend on any one given item. Parents: sit down before the vacation with your kids and go over what their souvenir limits are and remind them of those limits every time they want to purchase a souvenir.

Of course, the best way to set a souvenir limit and budget is to make the kids work for their Disney money: $2 for unloading the dishwasher or $1 for taking out the trash or $5 for making their bed every day for week. Little dollar amounts can add up over the course of weeks and months and the kids can have a nice nest egg built up by when it's time to leave for Disney.

You will have the best selection of souvenirs at the following locations: the Emporium on Main Street U.S.A. in Magic Kingdom, MouseEars in Future World at Epcot, and the World of Disney in Disney Springs. The best selection of mouse ears is at Chapeau Hat Shoppe on Main Street U.S.A. and Edith and Adrian's Head to Toe on Hollywood Boulevard in Hollywood Studios. Both locations will embroider the ears on site for you to pick up later in the day.

One of the nice benefits of staying on Disney property is the ability to ship souvenirs from the parks back to your resort. Anything shipped to your resort will be shipped to that resort's gift shop the next day, e.g., Wednesday for any souvenirs purchased in the parks on Tuesday. The resort gift shop will hold them until you pick them up. The only day you can't advantage of this service is on the final day of your vacation (you don't have a room to ship them back to). On this day, any souvenirs that you purchase must be carried with you throughout the park, so make sure those souvenirs are small and easy to carry.

Photography

Taking pictures is an important part of any Disney World vacation. However, there are a lot of written and unwritten rules to taking pictures in the parks. One of the most important written rules is new. During the late spring/

early summer of 2015, Disney banned selfie sticks from all Disney parks around the world. If a selfie stick is found at security or by a cast member inside the park, the guest will be instructed to leave and return their selfie stick to their car or resort room. Cameras mounted on monopods are permitted provided the guest follows the rule that all arms, legs, feet, and hands must remain inside the ride vehicle.

Since cameras are permitted inside the parks, the next most important rule is no flash photography on the attractions. This is especially important on dark attractions like "it's a small world", Peter Pan, and Under the Seas with Nemo and Friends. The flash from your camera can reflect off the attraction and back into other guests' eyes, temporarily blinding them, which will take away from the experience. There is enough light on these attractions for you to take plenty of good pictures without using a flash.

Many of the unwritten rules of Disney photography take place outside the attractions. Since selfie sticks have been banned from the parks, it's harder to get that picture of you in front of your favorite attraction, Disney landmark, or Cinderella Castle. The best thing to do is to ask another member of your party to take your picture. If you are by yourself, ask a passerby to take your picture. People will be more than happy to snap your picture and hand back your phone or camera. If you are uncomfortable asking a passerby, Disney has plenty of PhotoPass photographers who will take your picture with their camera and transfer it to your MagicBand so you can view it. They will also take your picture with any other camera that you hand them.

Another unwritten rule that can be applied for taking photos and just in general in the parks is to keep walking and stop only when you see other people taking pictures. If you must stop to take a picture in the middle of a walkway, take a glance behind you to see if anybody is walking close behind you that could walk into you. Disney World is a busy place even during slow times.

The last unwritten rule comes into play during parades and fireworks. During these events, it is okay to take some pictures during the pre-show and a couple of shots during the show. However, do not live behind your camera. It can become a distraction to guests around you and you could block their view of the show by constantly taking pictures. I was in Disneyland in August 2015 and had staked out a good spot to watch the nighttime shows until somebody claimed space in the row in front of me and proceeded to take pictures and videos of the parade with his iPad which obstructed my view. I was able to view the parade through his iPad, but it was not the view that I had expected for the show.

In the first unwritten rule, I mentioned PhotoPass Photographers. These photographers provide a great service to guests. They are stationed throughout the park, at select character meals, and at attractions to take pictures. You can purchase a package called MemoryMaker which will keep all of the vacation pictures that are scanned to a MagicBand which is linked to MemoryMaker account. This service costs $149 if purchased within three days of the start of your Disney vacation. The cost increases to $169 if purchased in the parks for immediate use. When you get home, you can view all of the pictures which may include some "Magic Shots" that PhotoPass photographers take during your vacation.

CHAPTER TWO

Magic Kingdom

Welcome to the park that started it all in Orlando, Florida. The Magic Kingdom opened for guests on October 1, 1971, and has grown year after year after year. Now, just over 19 million guests visit the Magic Kingdom in a calendar year, making it the most visited theme park in the world. The park itself is made up of six themed areas around a central hub where you can find Cinderella Castle and then head off into the different themed areas.

10 is a good age because you can start riding rides by yourself instead of sitting with a grown up every time. When you have a bigger family like us that means we can all ride because Mom and Dad have to sit with your brother and sister.
— Corbin Witlse, 11

MAIN STREET USA

Walt Disney World Railroad
Train Attraction : 20 minutes : No Height Restriction

This attraction can be found just inside the main gates to the Magic Kingdom. The Walt Disney World Railroad takes you on a 20-minute tour of the park with stops in Frontierland and Fantasyland. It is a great way to get the "lay of the land" if you have never been to the Magic Kingdom. Since it is only a 20-minute tour, it does not take much time out of your touring plan if you decide to go on a full tour. The railroad can also be used to rest your feet as it provides easy access to Frontierland and Fantasyland at the rear of the park.

Waits for the Walt Disney World Railroad are generally not very long. Except for busy times, you only have to wait for the next train to arrive before boarding. This attraction is not eligible for FastPass+ reservations.

Educational Slant: Where else can you find trains inside the Magic Kingdom? What made Walt Disney love trains so much? Can monorails be used as "the train of tomorrow"?

Town Square Theater

Meet-and-Greet Location : Time will Vary : No Height Restriction

Mickey Mouse is working "behind the curtain" getting ready to meet you. However, you can still meet him back there in this one-of-a-kind location. This Mickey Mouse interacts with guests calling them by name and having a brief conversation with them. How does Mickey do this? A good magician does not reveal all of his tricks, so good luck trying to get that information out of him.

This is a good attraction to go to right when the park opens as everyone heads to more popular attractions, and shortly before the park closes in the evening as everyone is leaving. This attraction is eligible for FastPass+ reservations which would be best used in the middle of the day.

Also in the Town Square Theater is Tinker Bell as she is tinkering in her shop and making pixie dust for all the guests. This is a separate queue from meeting Mickey Mouse so you will need to meet Mickey Mouse before entering the line to meet Tinker Bell. This theater is a great way to meet popular characters with great interactions with guests and manageable wait times.

Educational Slant: Was Mickey Mouse the first character that Walt Disney created? If not, who was? What helps make Mickey Mouse and Tinker Bell popular?

ADVENTURELAND

Swiss Family Tree House
Walkthrough Attraction: Time May Vary : No Height Restriction

Travel back to the 19th century with the Robinsons as they let you explore their treehouse after they became shipwrecked in the South Seas. You are able to explore the entire house from living room to the Crow's Nest to finally the Jungle Lookout. The Jungle Lookout gives you a 360-degree view of both Adventureland and the Magic Kingdom. You will have a great view of the boats sailing on the Jungle Cruise from this perch which requires you to climb 116 steps (6 stories) to reach.

There's rarely has a wait because you can walk on the attraction itself whenever you like. Once in the treehouse, you are able to explore at your own pace the different rooms and regions of the treehouse. This attraction is not available for FastPass+ reservations.

Educational Slant: Where were the South Seas and were they dangerous? Were there a lot of shipwrecks in this region of the world? Does today's technology make it easier to find people involved in shipwrecks?

Magic Carpets of Aladdin
Spinner Attraction : 1 Minute 30 Seconds : No Height Restriction

Riders are whisked away to the magical world of Aladdin as they hop on the magic carpets and spin around Adventureland. This ride is very similar to Triceratops

Spin in Animal Kingdom and Dumbo in Fantasyland. You will jump into a magic carpet and have the ability to control how high the carpet flies (front row) while guests in the back row control the pitch of the carpet. As opposed to spinning around a circus big top on Dumbo, Magic Carpets of Aladdin spins around a genie bottle. Camels located on the perimeter of the attraction will spit water on the riders as they pass by.

This attraction, typically, does not have long wait times. FastPass+ reservations are available, but I do not recommend getting them.

Educational Slant: Aladdin takes place in the fictional world of Agrabah. What real-life location or locations is the fictional world based on? Do genies exist? If not, where does the genie myth come from?

Enchanted Tiki Room: Under New Management

Show Attraction : 10 Minutes : No Height Restriction

You are transported to a world where Tiki birds have the ability to talk and sing. The birds take you through a 10-minute show of dialogue and song. There are over 225 audio-animatronic birds in this show who are led by the four bird conductors. You will enjoy this trip to Polynesia and will leave with the "Tiki, tiki, tiki, tiki, tiki room" song in your head for the rest of the day.

Waits to get into this show are not very long. The waiting area, like most, is standing ("no sitting on the handrails, please"). You have a large theater to find a seat and enjoy the show. FastPass+ reservations are not available.

Educational Slant: Research some of the birds in the show. How realistic are the audio-animatronic birds? Can some of these birds be trained to talk? If so, how?

Jungle Cruise

Boat Ride Attraction : 7 Minutes : No Height Restriction

Get ready to hop aboard the Jungle Cruise, a funny tour through the jungle. You will be able to see a diverse range of audio-animatronic jungle animals as they head down the river. You will also be able to see the mythical "back side of water". There are 15 different boats that you can ride. Each is named after a different river in the world. The overall theme of the cruise is that you are transported back to an old British jungle outpost. During the Christmas season, the cruise is "re-themed" as the Jingle Cruise.

This is one of the most popular attractions in Adventureland. You can expect wait times that increase throughout the day and never really go down until late in the evening. This attraction is available for FastPass+ reservations and they're recommended.

Educational Slant: Take a look at the top of your cruise ship; what river is it named after? Where is that river located? What cities does that river run through? How were rivers the lifeline of early civilizations?

Pirates of the Caribbean

Boat Ride Attraction : 8 Minutes 30 Seconds : No Height Restriction

Pirates lurk around every corner of this attraction which takes you on the high seas in a blend of classic Pirates of the Caribbean and the Disney movie series of the same name. You will see and hear the voices of your favorite characters during this eight-and-a-half minute journey. You will experience mermaids, hurricanes, ghosts of deceased pirates, and plunging down a short waterfall.

This attraction is the most popular one in Adventureland. Wait times start out long and only get longer throughout the day. FastPass+ reservations are available and highly recommended. Pirates of the Caribbean underwent a refurbishment in the summer of 2015 after an incident involving a guest placing their hand in the water. The guest lost part of a finger in the process. So please, keep arms and legs inside the boat at all times!

Educational Slant: Why did groups of people band together and become pirates? Could pirates in the 16th through 18th century be considered terrorists under today's definition of the word? Were there advantages to being a pirate?

FRONTIERLAND

Splash Mountain

Boat Ride Attraction : 11 minutes : Must be 40 Inches Tall

"YOU'RE GONNA GET WET!" is a common phrase heard on this attraction based on the movie *Song of the South*. You will enter their boat carved out of a log and join Br'er Rabbit as he attempts to avoid Br'er Bear and Br'er Fox who want to make the rabbit their dinner. This attraction has three drops. There are two minor drops during the indoor portion and a large drop (50 feet) at the end during which the logs reach a speed of 40 miles per hour. You will get wet on this drop before they enter the final scene where Br'er Rabbit celebrates his escape from Br'er Bear and Br'er Fox.

This is a popular attraction especially on hot days or during the middle of the day. FastPass+ reservations are available. However, if you can get to this attraction early in the day or at night when fewer people are willing to get wet, you should not have a long wait. A FastPass+ is a nice thing to have, but not a necessity.

Educational Slant: What causes the boat to go from zero to 40 miles per hour in only 50 feet? What era does *Song of the South* take place in? How would the story be different if the actors were people instead of animals?

Tom Sawyer Island

Walkthrough Attraction : At Your Own Pace : No Height Restriction

This is two attractions in one. You must hop on the log raft and float out to Tom Sawyer Island. Once on the island, there is plenty to explore and do. You can investigate Harper's and Potter's Mill or Injun Joe's Cave or even Tom Sawyer's Fort (which is specifically designed for guests aged 12 and younger). This is a great attraction for more timid guests while others in the party are riding Splash Mountain and Big Thunder Mountain Railroad.

The only wait time for Tom Sawyer Island is for a log raft to take you to or from the island. There is plenty of room to spread out and explore once on the island. FastPass+ reservations are not available.

Educational Slant: How close does the attraction lineup with the story of Tom Sawyer? Were log rafts a safe form of transportation on the river? What was considered safe transportation on the river?

Big Thunder Mountain Railroad

Roller Coaster : 3 Minutes 25 Seconds : Must be 40 Inches Tall

Hop aboard a runaway train from the Big Thunder Mining Company. Your train runs through the 19th century Gold Rush in the west. This mountain is almost 200-feet tall. The train takes you on a twisting and turning ride through the mining town. There are a few decent-sized drops, but nothing like the drop on Splash Mountain. You can also get a totally different experience riding the attraction at night as opposed to during the day. At night, the twists, turns, and drops are harder to see and, as a result, harder to prepare for. It is worth trying to ride both during the day and at night.

This is a very popular attraction. Guests, especially in the morning, will choose Big Thunder Mountain Railroad over Splash Mountain, so the wait times will build up faster here. Wait times are highest during the middle of the day and at night. FastPass+ reservations are available and highly recommended.

Educational Slant: How did people hear about the Gold Rush in the 19th century? How did people get out to California to participate in the Gold Rush? Was everyone successful at finding gold? What techniques did people and companies use to find the gold?

I like to ride Splash Mountain followed by Big Thunder Mountain Railroad. I call that the "wash and dry cycle".
— Julia Abrams, 16

Country Bear Jamboree

Show Attraction : 16 minutes : No Height Restriction

One of the original Magic Kingdom attractions, Henry the Bear acts as the host of the show which revolves around the concept of a traveling band of singing bears. There are lot of audio-animatronic bears and other animals that take part in the show. A different curtain opens when each group of bears performs their number. The show moves along rather quickly with lots of humor and back-and-forth banter among the bears.

Like a lot of show attractions, the only wait is for the next show to begin. The show does not have FastPass+ reservations available. This attraction is mainly a walk-up.

Educational Slant: How do the Country Bears differ from traveling bands from the 19th and early 20th century? How are do their make-shift instruments work? Are they like their real-life counterparts?

LIBERTY SQUARE

Liberty Square Riverboat

Boat Ride Attraction : 17 Minutes : No Height Restriction

Hop aboard the *Liberty Belle* and take a tour on the Rivers of America in Magic Kingdom. The *Liberty Belle* takes a half-mile tour around Tom Sawyer Island and is a great way to escape the crowds or get into the shade for a period of time. There is only one pick-up and drop-off point for the riverboat. Once you are on the boat, you are on the whole 17-minute journey. There are not a lot of seats on the boat. The best place to get a good view of Frontierland and parts of Adventureland is from the top deck. The best place to get out of the sun is on the middle deck while the bottom deck is the best place to find a seat.

The *Liberty Belle* holds 450 people and the only wait is for it to make its way around the Rivers of America/ Tow Sawyer Island loop. FastPass+ reservations are not available. The riverboat is a nice way to get out of the sun and away from the crowds during the middle of the day.

Educational Slant: Riverboats were once the life blood of America. How did they help America during the early Industrial Age? Where were riverboats most helpful? How did canals help end the age of the riverboat?

The Hall of Presidents

Show Attraction : 23 Minutes : No Height Restriction

Morgan Freeman narrates this 23-minute show which is part film, part narration, and part audio-animatronics. The show takes you on a brief tour of United States history. This show is based on Disneyland's Great Moments with Mr. Lincoln. The attraction has one of the most historical pre-show areas in Disney World. There are lots of presidential memorabilia and other items from the presidents and White House in the pre-show waiting area. The show ends with Morgan Freeman introducing each president.

The theater is very large and, as a result, the only wait, typically, is for the next show to begin. No FastPass+ reservations are available. This is another excellent attraction to get away from the crowds or mid-day sun. It's a long show and can provide a lot of relief from the heat while re-energizing you for more time in the Magic Kingdom.

Educational Slant: Pick a president and learn more about his time in office. What accomplishments did he have? What were his failures? Was he a successful president?

Haunted Mansion

Dark Omnimover Attraction : 7 Minutes
: No Height Restriction

There are 999 happy haunts awaiting you inside the Haunted Mansion. Is there room for one more? Are you brave enough to find out? The Haunted Mansion takes you on a spooky tour through its many rooms, each filled with a different variety of ghost. Some want to make the room seem a lot smaller or longer than the room really appears, others want to just hang out in the graveyard, while others want to host a séance to make more ghosts appears. Be careful when leaving the mansion; there are some "hitch-hiking ghosts" who want to come home with you.

This is the most popular attraction in Liberty Square. During busy times, waits can stretch over an hour. FastPass+ reservations are available and recommended, but the stand-by queue is one of the most unique and interactive in Magic Kingdom. Maybe there are some ghosts in this queue who want to come home with you as well.

Educational Slant: What makes people believe in ghosts and haunted buildings? Are ghosts more of a myth or a fact in our culture? What about in other cultures?

FANTASYLAND

It's A Small World

Boat Ride Attraction : 13 Minutes : No Height Restriction

Another original Magic Kingdom attraction from when the park opened in 1971. "it's a small world" transports you around the world to see different cultures through scenes of play, life, love, and song. You will see one of the biggest displays of audio-animatronics in the world as each country has brightly decorated audio-animatronics in its "mini-pavilion". You should be on the lookout for some of the unique animals in the show like the flower spotted hippo and the duck-billed platypus.

As an original Magic Kingdom attraction, guests both young and old enjoy "it's a small world". The result is a queue which can get long at times even for an attraction which can put a lot of people in each tour boat. FastPass+ reservations are available. While they wouldn't be my first choice for a FastPass+ reservation, those guests who are feeling nostalgic for the attraction or those who have younger children may want to make that reservation.

Educational Slant: How does the attraction show guests that even though cultures may appear to different, they may actually be more similar than once thought?

Peter Pan's Flight

Omnimover Attraction : 3 Minutes : No Height Restriction

Fly over London in your magical pirate ship and experience Peter Pan's Flight. You will fly over the story of Peter Pan as opposed to riding on the ground. So, guests who have a fear of even the slightest fear of heights should be aware of this before going on. Once on the attraction, fly to Neverland with Peter Pan and re-enact his story with the Darling family. You will have a different perspective of the scenes from above and the detailing of the scenes is done with this in mind. You will be able to see the depth of the actors and the scenery of London and Neverland.

This is one of the most popular attractions in Fantasyland. You will run to this attraction early in the morning. As a result, long wait times will quickly occur. Unless you able to get on this attraction either early in the morning or late at night, a FastPass+ reservation will be needed to help keep your wait to a minimum. It is not uncommon for wait times to exceed an hour.

Educational Slant: How has London changed from when the story of Peter Pan took place? What has not changed in London since the story took place? Would you rather live in "Old London" or "New London"? Why?

Mickey's PhilharMagic

Show Attraction : 12 Minutes : No Height Restriction

Donald steals Mickey's sorcerer's hat, but the orchestra instruments revolt against him setting the stage for Mickey's PhilharMagic. The hat, with Donald in pursuit, takes off on a journey through some of Disney's finest musical films and musical numbers. You will hear songs from *Beauty and the Beast*, *Aladdin*, "The Sorcerer's Apprentice" scene from *Fantasia*, *Peter Pan*, *The Little Mermaid*, and *The Lion King*. The pre-show area is a must-see, with Broadway-style posters of Disney musical acts throughout the area and music from *Fantasia* playing in the background.

This show does accept FastPass+ reservations, but, unless it is a peak time (mid-day through early evening), a reservation is not necessary. This is a great attraction to see at the beginning or the end of your time in Magic Kingdom. It is a 3D attraction, so 3D glasses are required to best experience the show.

Educational Slant: How many instruments make up an orchestra? How does the conductor keep all the instrument players in-line during a performance? Is performing in an orchestra something that you would want to do? If so, what instrument would you like to play?

Prince Charming Carrousel

Carrousel Attraction : 2 Minutes : No Height Restriction

Guests aged 2 to 92 will enjoy this spin on an early 20th century carrousel. This attraction greets people after they walk through Cinderella Castle and before they go deeper into the Fantasyland section of Magic Kingdom. Built in the 1910s, this carrousel features 90 wood-carved horses and one wood-carved chariot for you to ride on. The attraction spent most of its early years at Belle Isle Park in New Jersey before moving to the Magic Kingdom in time for opening day in 1971. There is one horse with a golden bow on its tail. That horse is rumored to be Cinderella's horse.

Because of its short ride duration and quick loading and unloading process, this attraction rarely has a wait longer than 10 to 15 minutes, even on crowded days in the park. There is no height restriction, so everyone in the Magic Kingdom is welcome to ride. There are no FastPass+ reservations available.

Educational Slant: How long did it take to carve one of these carrousel horses? How many people worked on the project to get the carrousel up and running in 1917?

The ride I would go to first is the carousel in Magic Kingdom because it really brings in magic around Fantasyland because it's circular.

— Carter Witlse, 9

The Many Adventures of Winnie the Pooh

Omnimover Attraction : 3 Minutes 15 Seconds : No Height Restriction

Travel through the Hundred Acre Wood with Winnie the Pooh and his friends. You enter this attraction riding in one of Winnie the Pooh's honeypots as they journey into the Hundred Acre Wood, meeting Tigger, Eeyore, Rabbit, and Owl as you bounce from room to room. One of the rooms has simulated thunder and lightning, so children who are afraid of that may be afraid of this room as well.

This is one of the more popular attractions in Fantasyland. It's not quite as popular as Peter Pan's Flight or the Seven Dwarfs Mine Train. That being said, lines will get fairly long, especially as the day goes on. However, Winnie the Pooh has one of the most interactive queues in Fantasyland. Kids can play in Rabbit's Garden, draw on the honey wall, or see if Piglet is home. A FastPass+ reservation is nice to have, but not a requirement.

Educational Slant: Is Winnie the Pooh real or part of Christopher Robin's imagination? Is having an active imagination a good thing or a bad thing? Would Magic Kingdom exist if Walt Disney didn't have dreams?

Mad Tea Party

Spinning Cups Attraction : 1 minute 30 seconds : No Height Restriction

Dash behind the looking glass into the Mad Hatter's Tea Party. You will jump into a tea cup and attempt to spin them as fast as you can as your tea cup moves around the attraction. Like the Haunted Mansion, there is a version of the Mad Tea Party at every Disney theme park throughout the world. Guests who get motion sickness easily may want to avoid this attraction because of its spinning nature.

Mad Tea Party has a quick loading and unloading process. As a result, there is rarely a long wait. The attraction is eligible for FastPass+ reservation, though with the short wait times, you don't really need one.

Educational Slant: How does the tea cup spin? What force is pushing the tea cup passengers to the outside of the tea cup? If the cup spins very, very fast,what can happen to the human body? Would people begin to black out?

Dumbo the Flying Elephant

Flying Attraction : 1 minute 30 seconds
: No Height Restriction

This attraction doubled in size and moved locations when Fantasyland expanded. Dumbo is located in the Storybook Circus section of Fantasyland. A second Dumbo attraction was added which spins in the opposite direction of the original attraction. Both are exactly the same with the same number of Dumbos on each side. The Dumbos work the same way, with a center joystick controlling how high or low the Dumbo flies. The attraction ends with all Dumbos flying at their highest altitude before coming back down to earth.

In between the two attractions, there is a large circus-themed play area where the kids can play while the parents wait for their "restaurant-style" pager to go off, telling them that it's time to ride. The attraction is available for FastPass+ reservations. Those guests do not have to wait in the play area, but can go right to the attraction. Because of its popularity with younger children, Dumbo will experience longer wait times during the morning and early afternoon.

Educational Slant: What and who made Dumbo believe he could fly? Is Dumbo a story of how people can achieve their dreams if they believe in them?

The Barnstormer

Low-Thrill Roller Coaster : 1 Minute 30 Seconds : No Height Restriction

Climb aboard The Barnstormer with Goofy and his friend as they take you on a journey riding this "introductory level" roller coaster. This attraction is great for both kids and adults who are trying to ease themselves or their children onto more thrilling attractions. The drops and turns are not too severe. The downside for the thrill-seeking type is the attraction is not very long at only 90 seconds of ride time.

This attraction is available for FastPass+ reservations. These reservations can come in handy to make the wait shorter during the busier times of the day (late morning and middle afternoon). This is another good attraction to go on either first thing in the morning or later in the evening and save those FastPass+ reservations for more popular attractions. There is no height restriction, so kids of all ages are welcome.

Educational Slant: Were there real-life barnstormers? What type of people were barnstormers and when were they at the peak of their popularity?

Under the Sea ~ Journey of the Little Mermaid

Omnimover Attraction : 4 Minutes : No Height Restriction

Ariel is looking for some friends to join her under the sea on this attraction themed after *The Little Mermaid* movie. You climb into a clam-shell and are welcomed by Scuttle from the movie as you enter the main part of the attraction. Once aboard the vehicle, you will enjoy a retelling of the basic story from *The Little Mermaid*. The best room, in my opinion, is where you enter the large dance-hall style room where fish and mermaids alike break out into song.

From there, you see different scenes from the movie which ends with Ariel and Eric's wedding.

The wait times for this attraction are difficult to judge. On one hand, it is an omnimover attraction which can move a lot of guests through the line. But it is a fairly new attraction, based on a popular movie, and so it draws in a lot of guests. Wait times can be described as "variable". The attraction is available for FastPass+ reservations and as one of the more popular attractions in Fantasyland, I would recommend them, but they are not a top priority.

Educational Slant: Is King Triton an over-protective father? Does his over-protectiveness help Ariel during the movie? What happens when King Triton is no longer over-protective toward Ariel?

Enchanted Tales with Belle

Show Attraction : 5 Minutes : No Height Restriction

This is a must-do attraction very early in the morning or late in the evening. The show is not long and the theater is not large, which can lead to long waits developing quickly. This show does have FastPass+ reservations which are a must-have if you have a Belle or Beast fan in your party.

Educational Slant: The story of Beauty and Beast takes place in 17th/18th century France. What was life like back in those times? Would a woman, like Belle, be encouraged or discouraged to read books? Why?

Seven Dwarfs Mine Train

Roller Coaster : 2 Minutes : No Height Restriction

HEIGH-HO! The Seven Dwarfs Mine Train is the newest attraction at the Magic Kingdom. The best description of the thrill level for this attraction is: it's more thrilling than Barnstormer but not as thrilling as Big Thunder Mountain Railroad or Space Mountain. The train cars have the ability to sway back and forth as they travel down the track. You also enter the caves where the Seven Dwarfs go during the day to mine for jewels. Unlike previous attractions with the Seven Dwarfs, there is very little Snow White in this one.

This is an attraction that people rush to as soon as the park opens in hopes of reducing their wait time. Unless you can outsprint a majority of the people to the front of the queue, you are better off using one of your FastPass+ reservations. Wait times get long quickly and stay long throughout the day, even into the later evening hours.

Educational Slant: What type of jewels did the dwarfs mine? Do you think that they were successful miners? How does the train car have the ability to sway from side to side? Do you think more roller coasters will use this technology in the future?

> *Seven Dwarfs Mine Train because they have*
> *some of the songs that are in the movie.*
> — Maureen Brooks, 10

Princess Fairytale Hall

Character Meet and Greet : Time May
Vary : No Height Restriction

Spend some time with a princess at Princess Fairytale Hall, a royal celebration set up much like the Town Square Theater. There are two options: Cinderella and Rapunzel or Anna and Elsa from *Frozen*. Cinderella/Rapunzel have their own queue and Anna/Elsa have theirs. Each area is wonderfully themed specific to the princess and her wants and needs and all the characters are human characters, not "head" characters like Mickey, Minnie, etc.

Anna and Elsa, due to the popularity of *Frozen*, have a much longer queue than Cinderella and Rapunzel. Though the wait for Anna and Elsa has dropped from the four to six hours during the early debut of Princess Fairytale Hall.

I recommend FastPass+ reservations, especially for the Anna and Elsa queue. Cinderella and Rapunzel have a more manageable queue, but there still can be some long wait times, especially during the middle of the day.

Once the Frozen section of the Norway Pavilion at Epcot opens, Anna & Elsa will be leaving Princess Fairytale Hall and moving to Norway. No word on what princesses will be replacing Anna & Elsa.

Educational Slant: There are still princesses in other countries around the world. What are some other countries that still have royalty? Is "being a royal" the same today as it once was? What has changed? What has stayed the same?

TOMORROWLAND

Tomorrowland Speedway

*Racing Car Attraction : 5 Minutes : Must be
32 inches to ride and 54 inches to drive*

You hop into a gas-powered race car which, unfortunately, can reach a top speed of seven miles per hour around the half-mile track. This low top speed is for everyone's safety since there are younger drivers, many of whom do not have a driver's license, going around the track. Another safety feature is the rail which the car rides upon. This rail does not allow the car to switch lines and cut-off, block, or cause an accident with another driver. These accidents would only slow the attraction down, causing longer wait times. It is still a fun attraction for the entire family and gives the younger drivers their first chance to be behind the wheel.

Because most of the queue is outside and uncovered, this is an attraction to experience in the morning or after the sun goes down. Waiting in the afternoon leaves you exposed to the sun beating down on you from above and the heat radiating off the track from below. This attraction is available for FastPass+ reservations. You must be 32 inches to be a passenger and 54 inches to be a driver.

Educational Slant: What safety measures are on today's race cars? Are there any race cars which are still "open cockpit" race cars like the ones on Tomorrowland Speedway? What kind of person does it take to be a race car driver?

Space Mountain
Indoor Roller Coaster : 2 Minutes 30 Seconds : Must be 44 Inches to Ride

This attraction is completely dark. The only light is the faint light given off by the stars inside the mountain. The drops are not as large when compared to other Disney World roller coasters, but the turns can feel more severe. In fact, everything feels faster and the drops and turns feel longer. Because you are inside with very little light, you can't see the track ahead of you and prepare for what is coming. Everything, especially for a first time rider, is a shock to the system because you don't know what is coming next. That is what makes Space Mountain one of Magic Kingdom's more popular attractions.

FastPass+ reservations are available and highly recommended. Space Mountain does not go out of service when thunderstorms roll through the Magic Kingdom, since the attraction is completely inside. There are long wait times throughout the entire day, even toward park close.

Educational Slant: How fast do you think the ship on Space Mountain is going? When you return from Disney World, compare your thoughts to the actual top speed and see how far off you were. How does the "unexpected" help increase the fear factor for this attraction?

I like Splash Mountain, Space Mountain, basically any attraction that has the word mountain in it.
— Maureen Brooks, 10

Astro Orbiter

Spinner Attraction : 2 Minutes : No Height Restriction

Soar high above Tomorrowland in your very own Astro Orbiter. This attraction, modeled after Dumbo, puts you 80 feet above Tomorrowland. Once in the Astro Orbiter, you have the ability to fly even higher using the joystick inside the orbiter. You do not have ground clearance to go "below 80 feet", so as not to scare guests on the ground with a low-flying orbiter. This is one of the more easily found and seen attractions in the Magic Kingdom due to its height.

The queue for Astro Orbiter is in two stages. The first stage is at ground level where you wait to board the elevator to the second stage. This is the longer of the two. The second stage is at the Astro Orbiter level. There are two elevators which transport guests up to this level. Most days, you would have to wait two or three cycles before boarding. The attraction is available for FastPass+ reservations, but they're not recommended due to the relatively short wait times.

Educational Slant: Would Astro Orbiters like these be possible someday? Will we be alive to see it? What inventions would need to occur to make these orbiters possible?

> *My favorite attraction is Astro Orbiter because*
> *I can tip my mom back and forth.*
> — Carter Witlse, 9

The Tomorrowland PeopleMover

Omnimover Attraction : 10 Minutes : No Height Restriction

Take a leisurely spin around Tomorrowland in the PeopleMover, or the Tomorrowland Transit Authority PeopleMover, as it's officially called. It takes you through some of the popular attractions of Tomorrowland. You'll take a journey into Space Mountain, zoom over the Tomorrowland Speedway, watch from above as others fight the Emperor Zurg, and get a glimpse of Walt Disney's original view for Progress City which transformed into Epcot.

This attraction just about never has a long wait. The cars on the PeopleMover can hold, depending on size, four to six guests. Plus, there are a lot of cars for people to ride. The PeopleMover is not available for FastPass+ reservations. Since the People<over has a short wait and a long ride time, I recommend this attraction for the middle of the day just to get out of the sun and to rest your feet.

Educational Slant: Could the PeopleMover technology be used in today's downtown areas? How? What cities, if any, have this kind of PeopleMover technology in use today?

Walt Disney's Carousel of Progress
Show Attraction : 22 Minutes : No Height Restriction

This is another attraction brought to Disney World from the 1964 World's Fair in New York City. The Carousel of Progress takes us through the story of everyday life in America. You follow one family through the 20th century and the advances which improved everyday life (and in some ways complicated that life). The fun part of the Carousel of Progress is that you rotate around a main center stage going from scene to scene.

This show is another great way to get out of the sun and rest your feet during the middle of your Magic Kingdom experience. It lasts 22 minutes and is air conditioned. It is also not a very popular attraction and rarely has a wait, so guests who need some extra rest can take in a second viewing of the show without leaving the theater. FastPass+ reservations are not available.

Educational Slant: What 20th century's inventions have made life easier? What inventions were designed to make life easier but ended up make life more difficult? What era of the 20th century would you like to live in, and why?

Buzz Lightyear's Space Ranger Spin

Shooter Attraction : 5 Minutes : No Height Restriction

The evil Emperor Zurg is attacking and it's up to a new cadet class of Space Rangers to stop him. This attraction is similar to Toy Story Midway Mania. There are many rooms where you shoot at targets to earn the top score. Space Ranger Spin is much more difficult than Toy Story Midway Mania. It is harder to see where you are aiming, the targets are smaller, and you are moving while trying to shoot. Don't be surprised if your score is lower on Space Ranger Spin than on Toy Story Midway Mania.

Space Ranger Spin is available to everyone with no height restriction. The attraction does have FastPass+ reservations. Like a lot of Disney attractions, FastPass+ reservations are a nice thing to have, but not a requirement. The attraction usually has short wait times early in the morning, late at night, and during traditional meal times. The queue is not very interactive, so if you are looking for entertainment, this is not the queue for you.

Educational Slant: Hitting a moving target is more difficult than hitting a stationary target. Why? Would this game be easier if the vehicle stopped and let you shoot at the target? How difficult would it be if the shooter stayed stationary but the targets moved?

Stitch's Great Escape

Semi-Thrill Attraction : 18 Minutes :
Guests Must Be 40 Inches to Ride

Experiment 626 (Stitch) has been brought to the Galactic Federation Prisoner Transport Center. Stitch is not happy with his capture, and wants to escape and get as far away from the transport center as possible. During his escape, Stitch will jump up and down on you, while "spitting" on them and burping food in their your to facilitate his escape. In the end, Stitch completes his great escape to Florida.

This attraction is very dark and loud which can be scary for some people. Guests must be 40 inches tall because of the restraints that come down on their heads. It takes place in a large theater so wait times are usually not a concern. FastPass+ reservations are available, but I do not recommend them.

Educational Slant: This attraction is an assault on the senses. How does the dark help heighten your senses? Do you depend more on other senses when you cannot see? How does your body compensate for the lack of sight?

Monsters Inc. Laugh Floor
Show Attraction : 10 Minutes : No Height Restriction

Join Mike Wazowski has he tries to fill the scream container with laugher. This is a fun interactive attraction where you are allowed to submit your jokes to be told during the show. The monsters will interact with the guests, asking them trivia to set up their joke or even flashing the camera on certain guests to get cheers or laughter from the rest of the crowd. Roz tells Mike throughout the show that he can't fill the can with laughter to power Monstropolis. Which will be more powerful: screams or laughter?

Like a lot of show attractions, Monsters Inc. Laugh Floor is in a large theater but not as large as some other theaters. As a result, you may have to wait a couple of shows before getting in. This attraction is not available for FastPass+ reservations. There are great interactions between the characters on screen and the guests. It's a better attraction when it is crowded because more people means more laughter and more fun!

Educational Slant: Laughter powers Monstropolis. In what ways does laughter help the human body?

CHAPTER THREE

Epcot

FUTURE WORLD EAST

Spaceship Earth

Omnimover Attraction : 15 Minutes : No Height Restriction

Spaceship Earth rising into the Florida sky is Epcot's center-piece attraction. It is the first one that you walk past after you enter Epcot through the main gates. Spaceship Earth tells the story of man's journey during their time on Earth. It starts in the early days of man before we had organized ourselves into a civilization and just hunted and gathered in packs. The attraction goes through the rise and fall of the Roman Empire, the Dark Ages, the Industrial Revolution, and the Computer Age before ending in the future. This is a great attraction in which to learn about our history.

Since it is the first attraction people walk past, human nature makes it the first one we want to ride. Even though Spaceship Earth is a continuous loading (omnimover) attraction, this rush of people will cause longer wait times in the morning. The best strategy is to ride in the middle of the day, especially after World Showcase opens and some foot traffic moves into that section of Epcot. The other option is to use one of your three daily FastPass+ reservations.

Educational slant: Spaceship Earth is filled with educational opportunities, from learning about the early days of man to the Roman Empire to the Industrial Revolution to imagining what the future holds for mankind. It is loaded with historical research and imagining the future.

Ellen's Energy Adventure

Show Attraction : 45 Minutes : No Height Restriction

Ellen DeGeneres leads you on a 45-minute adventure to learn about energy. The show begins with Ellen learning about how fossil fuels were formed. She then travels to the beginning of the universe at the Big Bang and learns more about the types of energy formed during that explosion and how those energy sources can be used to become power sources of the future. The show ends with Ellen using everything she's learned in a game of *Jeopardy!* against her old college rival. There are guest appearances from Bill Nye the Science Guy and Alex Trebek.

The show takes place in a large theater. The only wait time will be for the next show to begin. This attraction is not available for FastPass+ reservations, so the only way to see it will be to wait in line. Show times for the day can be found in the *Times Guide* located at the front of the park. This attraction is great during the hot summer months because it is a long show and can be used as a way to get out of the heat or late afternoon thunderstorm.

Educational Slant: This attraction is all about energy. Learn more about how fossil fuels were made, extracted from the earth, and then used. Learn about how we now burn fossil fuels "cleaner" than we did in the past. What sources of energy will be most beneficial to us in the future?

Mission: SPACE

Thrill Attraction : 6 Minutes : Must be 44 Inches Tall

Mission: SPACE, which is two attractions in one: a more thrilling orange side, and for those that still want to experience space travel to Mars with less turbulence, the green side. The orange side incorporates more spinning and violent motions. However, the objective of the attraction is the same for both sides: be part of an expedition crew traveling to Mars in hopes of colonizing the planet. Each module holds four people and each has a different task to complete in order for the journey to be a success. At the end of the attraction, you go out into the Advanced Training Lab. The training lab has other space-themed games for you to attempt and enjoy. Even those guests who did not go on Mission: SPACE are welcome to try their hand at the games.

Mission: SPACE (especially the orange side) is one of the attractions that people head to when they first enter Future World. While it doesn't hold the popularity of Test Track or Soarin', it will still cause a long line to form as the day goes on. As a result, FastPass+ reservations are available for the more intense orange side only. The tamer green side does not have the same long lines as the orange side.

Educational Slant: This is an attraction dedicated to the mission of space travel. Space travel is a relatively new compared to other forms of transportation. Learn about the pioneers of space travel and how they paved the way for modern forms of space travel. Should the U.S. still be in the business of exploring space? With the shutdown of the Space Shuttle program, there is no way for us to travel to space unless we "hitch a ride" with another country. Should the U.S. be looking into new forms of space travel?

Test Track

Thrill Attraction : 4 Minutes : Must be 40 Inches Tall

Test Track lets you experience what cars are subjected to by the manufacteurs and safety organizations before they hit the streets. On the current Test Track, you are able to design your own car before taking it out on the track. The attraction experience itself is only four minutes once you enter the car.

However, there is an extensive pre-show where you spend time designing your car before entering the "standing" part of the queue and then enter your car for the ride itself.

Once in their cars, you will enjoy the fastest attraction at Disney World as the car reaches a top speed of 65 miles per hour. Before reaching that top speed, you will have their car endure the rigors of the testing process. The car will go over severe bumps, deal with hot and cold temperatures, and dry/wet conditions. When the attraction is over, you can virtually take your car out on a series of mini-games in a showroom filled with the latest cars that GM has to offer.

Test Track does allow you to make FastPass+ reservations. I highly recommend that you do so. Wait times start out long and only get longer as the day wears on. So, unless your entire party can out-race people to Test Track, I would recommend getting a FastPass+ reservation.

Educational Slant: Since the attraction was refurbished, the explanation of the test track was taken out. What is a test track? What do car manufacturers learn by taking cars out on the test track? What would cars look like if there was no test track? What types of power sources can help cars be "greener?"

Test Track because you get to like make your own car and you race against someone else to see whose car is the best!
— Morgan Pouncey, 9

Innoventions East and West
Walkthrough Attraction : At Your Own Pace : No Height Restriction

Innoventions are/were two themed areas within Future World. Innoventions West closed for good on April 30, 2015, leaving just Innoventions East. The attraction is an indoor space filled with interactive games which help get kids moving. The highlight attraction of Innoventions

East is The Sum of All Thrills which allows you to create a roller coaster track. Then, the same robotic arm which created the track will take the guest on a simulated ride of the track that they created. The guest will experience the rises, drops, curves, rolls, and loops of their track.

Educational Slant: The attraction can be used to teach people about physics and what the body can and cannot handle when it comes to creating a roller coaster. What types of forces can the body endure? What can it not endure? What types of things do roller coaster designers need to think of when creating their roller coaster?

FUTURE WORLD WEST: THE SEAS

The Seas With Nemo and Friends

Omnimover Attraction : 4 Minutes : No Height Restriction

Board a "clam-mobile" for an undersea journey which tells the story of *Finding Nemo*. You will experience the EAC (East Australian Current) with Squirt and Crush. The scenes on the attraction are very life-like. Be sure to listen to Peach the Starfish at the end of the attraction; she always has something to say (number of clam-mobiles that have passed by, that music just keeps playing and playing, etc.)

The attraction has a really long queue, in terms of walking. The wait is generally very short. However, take some time and check out the queue as you walk through it. The queue takes you deeper and deeper under the sea. You start out seeing things that you typically see in the ocean, but as you go deeper you see things that you cannot see which survive only in deeper water. It is one of the better themed queues in Disney World.

This attraction does allow you to make a FastPass+ reservation. However, the wait times are generally not very long except during the middle part of the day.

Educational slant: What makes an omnimover attraction have shorter wait times compared to other attractions? Look at the fish in the queue which survive in the deeper water: what makes them able to survive with very little visible light getting down that deep? Could other fish or even humans live at those depths? How would we need to adapt?

Turtle Talk with Crush

Show Attraction : 10 to 16 minutes : No Height Restriction

Spend some time under the sea with Crush from *Finding Nemo*. This show is 10–16 minutes which is dependent on the interaction between Crush and the audience. Crush enters the tank and gives some facts about sea turtles, but he is more interested in the human world. Kids sit on the floor in front of the seating area while the adults sit in the back. Crush will ask for questions from both the kids and the adults (mainly the kids). Dory will stop by and visit Crush as well and the audience will help save both Dory and Crush from the whales. Once the show is over, the adults will find their little "squirts" and exit the theater.

This is a very popular attraction and the theater is not large. As a result, it is eligible for FastPass+ reservations. Unless you can make the first show of the day, get a FastPass+ reservation. It saves the trouble of possibly waiting for multiple shows to take place before you can in.

Educational Slant: How are sea turtles like Crush different from the turtles you see in a pond? How are turtles, in general, different from tortoises? How old do sea turtles get?

The Seas Exhibits

Walkthrough Attraction : At Your Own Pace : No Height Restriction

After getting off The Seas with Nemo and Friends, you enter the large area where The Seas Exhibits are located.

This vast area is filled with different aquariums which are home to a wide variety of fish and other sea mammals. Be sure to explore both floors of the exhibits. The aquariums are very tall to give the fish some room to spread out. You can also watch some short shows on feeding the fish, fish breeding, and other topics. See if you can find Nemo, Dory, and other fish from *Finding Nemo*.

Educational Slant: Pick a species of fish and research it. Where do they like to live? What do they like to eat? Are they endangered? If they are endangered, what is being done to save them from extinction?

FUTURE WORLD WEST: THE LAND

The Land is home to three attractions inside the main building and what was used to be two attractions outside the building. Captain EO ended its run in early spring 2015. The Captain EO Theater is currently being used to show extended previews of upcoming Disney and Pixar movies.

Soarin'

Thrill Attraction : 5 Minutes : Must be 40 Inches Tall

Soarin' takes you on a hang-glider like ride over California. You are placed into seats like those on inverted roller coasters. The floor drops away once all the guests are secured. It is a long attraction compared to most roller coasters, but California is a large state and you get to experience all that the state has to offer. The queue has been upgraded recently to be more interactive with short games for the people to play like the queue in Space Mountain, but outside of those games, don't expect a lot of things to hold your interest while waiting in the queue.

This is a very popular attraction. At park open, guests will sprint to opposite sides of the park to get in the queue for either Mission: SPACE, Test Track, or Soarin'. Mission:

SPACE and Test Track are both on the east side of Future World so that traffic does get divided up somewhat. Soarin' is the only popular attraction on the west side of Future World. Wait times start out long and get longer as the day goes on. Fortunately, Soarin' does have FastPass+ reservations. Like a lot of the popular attractions, either get to the attraction when the park opens or get a FastPass+.

On June 17, 2016, Soarin' Over California will reopen as Soarin' Around the World.

Educational Slant: How do the attraction experiences of Mission: Space and Soarin' differ? How are they the same? How does the uses of scents during Soarin' make you feel like you are in that location?

Be sure to get FastPasses for Soarin' - it's really relaxing after walking around Epcot, but the regular line is incredibly long.
— Kathryn Matt, 9

Circle of Life: An Environmental Fable

Show Attraction : 12 minutes : No Height Restriction

The Circle of Life is a story about how the world needs to conserve resources and how population growth is making the need for these precious resources very important. Viewers of the film are taken back to a time where the population was small and resources were plentiful and thought to be unlimited. As the movie continues, time moves on and we reach a point where the population is large. As a result, resources are scarce and we discover that some of those resources do have limits. The characters from *The Lion King* show people how to conserve and recycle (Circle of Life) some of those resources so that everyone may have a chance to use them. Parents, who went to Disney World as a child, see if you can spot the sequences of the film that were in the old movie showed in this theater: *Symbosis*.

The film for this attraction is shown on a continuous loop and, as a result, it does not have show times. You are free to enter and exit the theater as you please. There is rarely, if ever, a line to get in. There are no FastPass+ reservations.

This attraction is currently closed for refurbishment.

Educational Slant: What conservation efforts are ongoing in your community? What conservation efforts have you learned about during your vacation at Disney World? What resources on the Earth are unlimited? Have limits? What can be done to recycle the limited resources to extend their life?

Living With The Land

Boat Attraction : 15 minutes : No Height Restriction

Living with The Land is two attractions in one. The first is at the start of the boat ride when move through a human history of how we have lived with the land during our time on Earth. Be sure to wave to the people eating dinner at the Garden Grill as you pass by. After the history of our time with the land, you are taken back into the Disney greenhouses. In these greenhouses or "Living Laboratory", you learn about how to grow plants where there are scarce resources (like water) or fish farming, or how to grow crops from a variety of climate zones (tropical, temperate, etc.). This fun attraction teaches a lot of things about farming with limited resources. Plus, at least for the first part of the attraction, it's a good way to cool off. Once in the greenhouse, however, you feel some of the heat and humidity.

This attraction used to have shorter wait-times than it currently does now. Once FastPass+ was introduced, guests used Living With The Land as a way to kill time before their reservation window at Soarin' opens up since the two attractions are a short walk from each other. That said, wait times rarely exceed 15–20 minutes, though they will get long during busy times of the day like around lunch and dinner. Again, this is because it is a short walk from the food court. FastPass+ reservations are available.

Educational Slant: Research the methods used to grow plants with limited resources such as water. How does "fish farming" help increase the fish population in certain areas?

Living with the Land - I love the educational side to this ride. For me, being able to see things up close and personal makes me appreciate new ways to grow and develop food sources which is something I am very interested in. I love to listen to the background music from that ride even when we are at home.
— Kate Nicely, 10

Journey Into Imagination with Figment

Omnimover Attraction : 6 Minutes : No Height Restrictions

One of the original attractions at Epcot, it has undergone a lot of transformation and tweeking over the years to get to the attraction that it is today. However, the basic premise of the attraction has remained the same. You are loaded into an Omnimover car and transported to the land of imagination and dreams featuring Dr. Channing and his assistant, Figment. Figment is a purple dragon and one of the original mascots for Epcot. You journey through the five senses with Figment. Midway through the attraction, Figment derails the tour and takes you to his open house to see what happens when the imagination is truly set free before returning to the real world.

There is no height restriction for this attraction. Parents be aware that there are some loud noise and very foul smells which might trouble younger guests. FastPass+ reservations are available, though wait times are not long. Like Living with The Land, the wait times have gotten longer with the introduction of the FastPass+ reservation system.

Educational Slant: Let your imagination run wild. What does it come up with? Let your dreams guide you through this attraction.

WORLD SHOWCASE

The World Showcase is based around the concept that Walt Disney had for a permament World's Fair at one of his parks. Disneyland was surrounded by city development. Magic Kingdom already had an identity among park goers. Epcot, which opened in 1982, became the home of this permament World's Fair. The World Showcase has 11 countries (pavilions). Be aware, the World Showcase loop is long (over one mile). It's a lot of walking, but fortunately there are places to stop and take in the world.

Mexico

The first pavilion you will come across (if turning left at the end of Future World) is the Mexico Pavilion. Its signature structure is a large Aztec pyramid. Inside you will find a large open-air market featuring Mexican trinkets and other associated charms. One of Mexico's two sit-down style restaurants, San Angel Inn, is located here, too.

The Gran Fiesta Tour, also inside the pyramid, is an eight-minute ride through the countryside and history of Mexico. Donald Duck, one of the Three Caballeros, has gone missing and the other two caballeros (Panchito and Jose) must find him before their concert is scheduled to begin. This attraction does not have very long lines. Wait times are generally in the five to ten minute range. There are no FastPass+ reservations.

Outside the pyramid, you will find another sit-down style restaurant, La Hacienda de San Angel. You will also find a counter service restaurant, Cantina de San Angel. For entertainment, Mariachi Cobre will entertain you with their unique brand of Mariachi-style music. For younger ones and the young at heart, Donald Duck dressed in Mexican attire makes appearances for photographs just outside the pyramid.

Educational Slant: Research the Aztecs and why pyramids were so important to them. Go back and watch the film *The Three Caballeros* and write a review of the film.

Norway

The Norway Pavilion is is undergoing a lot of transition. The boat ride Maelstrom closed in 2014 to make way for a new attraction about Norway featuring the characters from the movie *Frozen*. There will also be a newly constructed area where you can meet Anna and Elsa from *Frozen*. The rest of the pavilion remains unchanged with classic Norwegian architecture throughout. The pavilion has plenty of shopping with a series of interconnected shops—a design feature seen throughout the World Showcase.

The headline restaurant is Akershus which serves food with a Norwegian flair. It is also the home of a princess meet and greet for breakfast, lunch, and dinner. Appearances by the princesses will vary by meal, with those present at breakfast may or may not be present at lunch or dinner. As a result, this is a highly sought after dining reservation, so plan accordingly.

There is also a bakery which serves a wide variety of Norwegian pastries and other baked goods. It is famous for its school bread which is a sweet roll with vanilla filling and a coconut topping.

Educational Slant: If you have seen the *Frozen*, compare the style of dress and architecture in the movie to the architecture in the pavilion. Or learn more about the Vikings and how the Vikings, at one time, were the most feared marauders in the world.

China

The China Pavilion has a similar set up to the Mexico Pavilion. You enter through the large Chinese gate and work your way back to the main portion of the pavilion. The main structure is the Temple of Heaven where you can watch *The Reflections of China*, a 13-minute film which features a tour of China's landscapes, cityscapes, and historical structures like the Great Wall of China. The film is presented in 360-degree Circle Vision; since it "surrounds" you, there may be things that you miss with just one viewing.

Outside the Temple of Heaven, there are two gift shops: one which features puppets and toys, the other housewares and other Chinese-themed household goods. There are also two restaurants. Nine Dragons is table-service, Lotus Blossom Café is counter-service restaurant. Both serve popular Chinese cuisine. For entertainment while walking the pavilion, you will see the Dragon Legend Acrobats, and Mulan will be available for photographs. Schedules for the Acrobats and Mulan vary from day-to-day.

Educational Slant: How long did it take to build the Great Wall of China? What makes it one of the Seven Wonders of the World? What is the history behind the Temple of Heaven? How is it important to Chinese culture?

Germany

Germany is our first "attraction-less" pavilion on the World Showcase. However, Germany makes up for it with excellent shopping and dining experiences. Also, it is home to the Miniature Train and Village. This mini-attraction was originally designed for the Epcot Flower and Garden Festival, but due to its popularity, it has become a year-round attraction for the pavilion.

The shopping areas wind their way through the Platz (German for "square"). These shopping areas focus on German-style teddy bears, sporting goods, and home wares. The most popular shopping area is Karamell-Kuche where hand-made German-style caramel candies and pastries are made. If you love caramel, then Karamell-Kuche is the shop for you.

Germany has table-service and counter-service style restaurants. The Biergarden has family-style seating where you will be placed next to other families at long tables. Cuisine is highly German with some American flair thrown in. The counter-service restaurant, Sommerfest, focuses on German sausage sandwiches with a traditional hot dog added in for those with simpler tastes.

Educational Slant: Look at the architure of the pavilion and when you get home learn more about it and what era it comes from. See if you can find the statue of St. George and the Dragon and learn the history of the story, where it comes from, and what it means to the German people.

Italy

Much like Germany, Italy is another attraction-less pavilion. But again like Germany, Italy makes up for it with lots of shopping and dining. There are two main shopping areas. The first, Il Bel Cristallo, focuses on high-end Murano glass, crystal, and porcelain. The other, La Bogetta Italiano, focuses on cookware and Italian food. There are other small shops sprinkled throughout the pavilion.

The pavilion has two sit-down restaurants. But they are very different. The first is the more formal (but not too formal) Tutto Italia. It has a very intimate feel, and the menu features Italian-style entrees like beef, chicken, and fish, and not so many pasta dishes.

When compared with Tutto Italia, the second sit-down restaurant, Via Napoli, has a much more open feel. It has both family-style long tables and individual tables. Its high ceilings spread out the noise in what can become a very loud restaurant. The high ceilings also reduce the impact of the heat coming off pizza ovens. This restaurant is known for its pizza. Water is shipped from Naples, every day, to help make the dough for the pizza which gives it a more Italian flavor. The restaurant also specializes in more pasta-style dishes than Tutto Italia.

When the Italy Pavilion was designed, a mix of designs were used in creating it, including Roman, Venetian, and Napleon styles of architecture.

Educational slant: Take note of architecture in the pavilion and see where one citys architecture ends and another begins. What is different about each city's architecture? Are there any similarities?

The American Adventure

The American Adventure is where Americans can "come home" to the United States. It has a colonial town feel, from the architecture to the signage to the attire of the cast members. Its 30-minute show attraction takes you on a crash course of United States history hosted by Benjamin Franklin and Mark Twain. The pre-show while waiting for the next showing to begin is not to be missed. Usually, the Voices of Liberty come out and sing patriotic songs to get people into the spirit of show.

The American Adventure pavilion is also home to the American Gardens Theater. This theater is used for the Candlelight Processional at Christmas time, along with other concerts and shows throughout the year.

There is a large cafeteria-style quick-service restaurant, The Liberty Inn, located inside the main building. The restaurant focuses on summer grill food like chicken sandwiches, hamburgers, and hot dogs. Also located in the main building is a gift shop. Outside the building are small kiosks serving a variety of snack food and drinks.

The American Adventure building is the largest one in the World Showcase at five stories tall, but it looks the smallest (only 2½ stories) because of the forced perspective used by the Disney Imagineers.

Edcuational Slant: You will spend a lot of time learning about US history in school. How did Disney Imagineers use forced perspective to make the main building look only half its actual size? Is this a common design technique?

Japan

Next, you're transported to the Far East and the Japan Pavilion. Japan is home to an attraction, two sit-down restaurants, a quick-service restaurant, and a large shopping area.

The attraction is Bijutsu-kan, a massive art gallery. The art is shown on a rotating basis. Like all of the other attractions in the World Showcase, there is no height restriction, but please keep your hands off of the art.

The two sit-down restaurants, Teppan Edo and Tokyo Dining, each focus on a different style of Japanese cuisine. Teppan Edo focuses more on stir-fried food and foods created in front of you like at teppanyaki restaurants. Tokyo Dining has a sushi focus but does have some grilled items on the menu. The lone quick-service restaurant is Katsura Grill with a lot of "grab-and-go" items on the menu.

The shopping area at the Mitsukoski Department Store is large and has everything under one roof. You will walk from one department to another. It's different from the other pavilions where the various shopping venus are broken up by store than by department.

Educational Slant: Compare the architecture of China to the architecture of Japan. For countries that are near each other, how is the architecture similar? How is it different? Learn about the Teppanyaki style of restaurant. How does it fit into the Japanese culture?

Morocco

Welcome to the only African country in the World Showcase: Morocco. Morocco is easy to spot with its open pavilion and nod to both the Spanish and French history of the country.

Morocco is also the only country to have the government, not a corporation, sponsor it. The King of Morocco sent workers over to work hand-in-hand with Disney to make sure that the décor of the pavilion fit the Moroccan culture. You will not find any artwork of people in the main building of the pavilion. Disney even made sure that the appearance of the Tower of Terror, which can be seen in the distance from the pavilion, fit with the Moroccan architecture.

The dining in Morocco is good and readily available. Restaurant Marrakesh serves traditional Moroccan cuisine. The other table-service restaurant, the Spice Road Table, is the newer of the two, and also serves traditional Moroccan cuisine, though you can find more grilled items on its menu. The quick-service restaurant is Tangerine Café where you can find more portable Moroccan cuisine like shwarmas and wrapped sandwiches. There is American cuisine items on the children's menu.

Educational Slant: What makes Morocco one of the more "European" African countries?

France

France is one of the best overall pavilions in the World Showcase. It has a little of everything. It has characters available to meet (Belle from *Beauty and the Beast* and Aurora from *Sleeping Beauty*). It has a wide variety of shops selling a wide variety of goods. There is a mini Eiffel Tower in the background overlooking the whole pavilion. You can enjoy an 18-minute film, *Impressions de France*, which takes you throughout the French countryside and cityscapes. The film has been running since Epcot opened on October 1, 1982. So, your parents probably remember seeing it when they were kids.

Food is all over this pavilion. You can find snack items at many small kiosks. There is a bakery which serves breakfast, lunch, and dinner. It opens when Future World opens, at 9 am. Before you get to the bakery, there is an excellent ice cream shop, L'Artisan des Glaces, and at the front of the pavilion, you will find the table-service restaurant, Chefs de France.

Educational Slant: What advancements has France made since the film was released in 1982? It's been a long time since its release. What scenes would you take out? What scenes would you add?

United Kingdom

You have to cross over a small bridge that goes over a body of water which some call the English Channel to get to the United Kingdom pavilion. The United Kingdom has no attractions, but does have a meet and greet with Mary Poppins (and sometimes one of her penguins). Depending on the day and time, you could also meet Alice from *Alice in Wonderland* as well as characters from *Winnie the Pooh*. There are plenty of shops from guests to get their shopping fix (sports, tea, historical crest research, etc.).

There is also a live band—British Revolution—which will play music from when the United Kingdom ruled the music scene in the 50s and 60s. They will play more "modern" music from the 70s through the 90s as well.

The United Kingdom Pavilion has excellent dining options. It has a counter-service option, the Yorkshire County Fish Shop, which serves fish and chips as well as British cookies from dessert. The fish and chips are served like they are served in the UK: on newspaper. The table-service option is The Rose and Crown Pub, which is a great place to get a reservation for later in the evening. The restaurant opens up the patio to customers so they can watch the Illuminations fireworks show at the end of the evening.

Educational Slant: Ask your server at the Rose and Crown Pub why it's called the Rose and Crown Pub. What made British music so popular in the 50s and 60s? What groups made it popular? How did those bands appearing in the United States help change music in America?

Canada

The World Showcase ends with a stop at our northern neighbors: Canada. This is a very lively pavilion with a little something for everyone. There is a lumberjack show featuring axe tossing and log rolling. Those not interested in the lumberjacks can spend some time over in the garden area modeled after the Butchart Gardens in British Columbia. After the show and some time in the garden, you can go see *O Canada!* a 360-degree CircleVision show which provides a glimpse into the Canadian way of life. The film is narrated by comedian Martin Short.

The food in Canada is all located in one restaurant, Le Cellier, a table-service restaurant focusing on steaks. Le Cellier is designed after a wine cellar in a building modeled after the famous Chateau Laurier in Ottawa, the Canadian capital. The restaurant is very small and the tables are close together, but that does not hide the fact that Le Cellier grills up one of the best steaks at Disney World. There is no counter-service restaurant in the Canada Pavilion.

Educational Slant: Research the Butchart Gardens and Chateau Laurier and compare them to the smaller-scale versions (Victoria Gardens and Hotel du Canada) located in the Canada Pavilion.

CHAPTER FOUR

Hollywood Studios

Hollywood Studios is the old Disney/MGM Studios. The idea behind the park is a working movie studio. This results in a confusing layout. Some areas of the park has only attraction (or even none at all) and others have three or more. In terms of thrill rides, however, Hollywood Studios has the highest ratio of thrill attractions to regular attractions of the four Disney World parks.

The Great Movie Ride
Boat Ride Attraction : 22 Minutes : No Height Restriction

The Great Movie Ride is a 22-minute journey through the history of film. There are some scary parts (simulated gunfire and aliens) which could scare younger children, so keep that in mind when planning. The Great Movie Ride will also be undergoing some renovations in the near future. Turner Classic Movies recently obtained the sponsorship of the attraction and will be adding/deleting scenes as well as adding both a new pre- and post-show.

This attraction is a great way for parents to introduce their children to some of the movies from their youth. It is a fun attraction and a great way to learn about the movies. There are no FastPass+ reservations.

Educational Slant: How was film-making different in the past compared to today? What made films longer to make compared to today? What innovations from film-making do we still use today?

Frozen Sing-A-Long
Show Attraction : 30 Minutes : No Height Restriction

Get transported to the Kingdom of Arendelle and join the cast of *Frozen* for a celebration of the movie through song. The cast of *Frozen* will take you through a re-telling of the movie filled with song and you are allowed to sing along with the cast.

This is a popular attraction, with showings throughout the day, and the stand-by line can get very long. FastPass+ reservations are available and I recommend them.

Educational Slant: How do the songs help tell the story? Do the songs form a mental picture of the movie?

Indiana Jones Epic Stunt Spectacular
Show Attraction : 25 Minutes : No Height Restriction

A lot of the stunts seen in this show can be seen in the *Indiana Jones* series of movies (another reason to see The Great Movie Ride attraction). The show also has some audience participation for some of the stunt scenes. There is one cast member planted in the audience who is always selected for the stunt scenes which require audience participation. Stunts are mainly taken from *The Raiders of the Lost Ark*, the first movie in the series.

The show takes place outdoors and guests are seated on bleachers, in the shade, but on hot days it will be tough to beat the heat. Also, as an outdoor show, the show will close when inclement weather, especially lightning, is in the area. There are many showings throughout the day—check the *Times Guide* for show times. The attraction does accept FastPass+ reservations though it is a large theater with seating for over 2,000 guests per show.

Educational Slant: What effects are used to accomplish the stunts? What safety mechanisms are in place to ensure the safety of the performers?

Star Tours

Thrill Attraction : 4 minutes 30 seconds
: Must be 40 Inches Tall

Star Tours takes you on a thrilling adventure through scenes of the *Star Wars* movies. The attraction is hosted by C3P0 who sends you on a simulated ride on a Starspeeder to escape the Rebel Alliance. There are 50 different scenes that you can experience, so it is rare to have the same experience twice. Some of the experiences simulate short rises and drops. Be sure to listen to the instructions on how to properly strap yourself into your seat for the experience. Also, watch out for your fellow travelers, as one of them is a Rebel spy, but they will not reveal themselves until the end of the experience.

This is a popular attraction within Hollywood Studios. It is especially popular during Star Wars Weekends in May and June. The attraction is eligible for FastPass+ reservations, but keep in mind that travelers under 40 inches tall cannot ride.

Educational Slant: Is space travel like that in *Star Wars* possible? What advances in science need to be made to make this type of space travel possible?

Muppetvision 3D

Show Attraction : 13 Minutes : No Height Restriction

Dr. Bunson Honeydew and Beaker take you behind the scenes at Muppet Labs where they have just unlocked the secrets of 3D. You enjoy a 13-minute show filled with puns and cheap 3D tricks as Waldo, the newly created 3D graphic, creates havoc during a taping of a vintage Muppet Show from the 1970s. You will be able to see all of the Muppet favorites, including Kermit, Miss Piggy, and Grover. The show ends with a "3-hour salute to all nations but mostly America" that you do not want to miss.

Muppetvision 3D, since it is held in a large theater, rarely has a long wait. Most of the time, you will just have to wait in the pre-show area, which is filled with props from *The Muppet Show*, for the next show to begin. FastPass+ reservations are accepted, but you don't need them.

Educational Slant: How does 3D work with the animation in MuppetVision? Does 3D film-making take longer to make than standard 2D film-making? If it does, what makes it take longer?

Toy Story Midway Mania

Shooting Attraction : 5 minutes : No Height Restriction

Guests of all ages will enjoy Toy Story Midway Mania. This attraction simulates carnival-style games and helps create competition amongst family members to see who can get the high score. You are loaded into a car with a "gun" to shoot at the targets during the various games, then you're taken through a series of "shooting" games hosted by different characters from the *Toy Story* films. Each game has a different theme and targets to shoot at. To help level the playing field, high scoring targets are at both high and low eye-level so the younger participants don't have to try to shoot upwards to get the high-scoring targets. At the end of the games, the scores are added up and a winner is declared in each car while the high scores for the past hour and for the day are displayed.

3D glasses are needed for this popular attraction. To minimize wait times, I recommend going on early in the day or making FastPass+ reservations. Wait times start out long and only get longer.

Educational Slant: What leads to high scores on this game? What makes hitting the targets worth higher scores difficult? What do the characters say and interact with the guests to make them go after the higher targets?

Walt Disney: One Man's Dream

Walkthrough Attraction with Film : 15 minutes (film) : No Height Restriction

Walt Disney: One Man's Dream gives you a closer look at the history of Walt Disney. The attraction is really two attractions in one. There is a large gallery featuring many items, from Walt Disney's childhood and life in Missouri to his early attempts at animatronics to his early plans for Disneyland. At the rear of the gallery, there is a theater which shows a 15-minute film about Walt Disney's life hosted by Julie Andrews. Seating in the theater is first-come/first-served.

Since this is a walkthrough attraction with no real queue, One's Man Dream is not eligible for FastPass+ reservations. On the flip side, as a walkthrough attraction, there is never a wait to get in or any difficulty finding seating in the theater. It's a good attraction to escape the heat of the days.

Educational Slant: What events in Walt's childhood helped form his ideas for Disneyland? In his early designs for the park, what things were changed? What things were added? What was removed? What attractions from the 1964 World's Fair can guests experience in Disney World today?

Voyage of the Little Mermaid

Show Attraction : 17 minutes : No Height Restriction

Voyage of the Little Mermaid is a show combining scenes from *The Little Mermaid*, live action, and puppets. The show retells the story of *The Little Mermaid*. You're treated to songs and dialogue from the movie. You'll be sprayed with mist from the ceiling during some parts of the show.

This is one of the more popular shows at Hollywood Studios, and the theater does not have a large seating capacity compared to other shows in the park. As a result, the queue to get in grows during the day, but starts to drop off later in the afternoon and evening. FastPass+ reservations are available.

Educational Slant: Where did the myth of the mermaid come from? How did it grow? Are mermaids still culturally significant in some countries?

Star Wars Launch Bay

Walkthrough Attraction : At Your Own Pace : No Height Restriction

Welcome to the newest attraction at Hollywood Studios. This area has taken over the former Animation Courtyard and made it your one-stop shop, so to speak, for all things Star Wars. You will be able to meet some past and present characters from the *Star Wars* movies and *Star Wars Rebels* TV series on Disney XD. You can also tour the launch bay and see up-close prop and costumes from the films. If you need to rest your feet, you can enter the Launch Bay Theater and watch a 10-minute film and get a behind the scenes look at the making of the *Star Wars* series. After that, you can play *Disney Infinity 3.0* with characters from the movies.

Educational Slant: *Star Wars* is a great study for the history of computer-aided design in film-making. How does the film-making from the original trilogy differ from the second and third trilogies? What advances were made? How can computer-aided design help trim or expand costs to a movie's budget?

Disney Junior Live on Stage

Show Attraction : 24 Minutes : No Height Restriction

The youngest guests to Disney World will love this show featuring their favorite characters from the Disney Junior Channel. You will enter a large sound stage and help the characters from *Mickey Mouse Clubhouse* celebrate Minnie's Birthday. The characters get some assistance from the stars of other Disney Junior shows and of course, Toodles, who helps in every episode of *Mickey Mouse Clubhouse*. At the end, everyone celebrates Minnie's birthday and there are gold doubloons and bubbles to pop for everyone.

There is no formal seating for this show. All of the seating is on the floor of the sound stages. There are a few benches at the rear for guests who do not wish to sit on the floor. This is a popular attraction, especially for toddlers and pre-schoolers. It is available for FastPass+ reservations. The theater is large, and even though you may see a long line, there is a good chance that you will be able to see the next show if you get in line. Shows take place throughout the day.

Current Disney Junior shows that participate in the attraction are *Jake and the Neverland Pirates*, *Doc McStuffins*, and *Sofia the First*.

Beauty and the Beast Live on Stage

Show Attraction : 25 Minutes : No Height Restriction

The show has been running since *Beauty and the Beast* debuted in theaters on November 22, 1991. It takes place at the Theater Under the Seats which holds 1500 guests. The show goes through the movie in a Broadway-style production. Songs from the movie with the original voice actors are grafted into the show. You will love seeing this stage production from one of the classic Disney movies.

You have the option of waiting in line or getting a FastPass+ reservation. The theater is large, so having a FastPass+ is not a requirement though they are a nice thing to have for the show.

Educational Slant: How well does the stage show capture the scenery of France? Do the songs help tell the story? How do they help replace traditional dialogue?

Rock 'n' Roller Coaster

Thrill Attraction : 5 Minutes (including pre-show): Must be 48 inches tall

You blast off into a roller coaster filled with music and cork-screw turns and inversions. This attraction has the fastest acceleration of all the Disney World attractions: 0 to 58 mph in only 2.8 seconds, with 4.5 G-forces. Throughout the attraction, you'll hear music from Aerosmith. Neon road signs with humorous messages are seen throughout as well.

This is one of more popular attractions at Hollywood Studios. The wait time builds quickly throughout the morning and afternoon. FastPass+ reservations are available are highly recommended. There is also a single rider line for guests who are going on the attraction by themselves.

Educational Slant: What are G-forces? How does rapid acceleration cause higher G-forces? How many G-forces can the human body handle? What happens to the body when it can no longer handle the G-forces pushing on it?

One thing I would really skip if you're a kid like me is Rock N Roller Coaster because it's a little too fast.
— Carter Witlse, 9

My favorite attraction is Rock N Roller Coaster because you can go really fast and the music takes the speed off your mind.
— Corbin Witlse, 11

I love Rock'n' Roller Coaster because it's in the dark and how fast it goes. I also love the music.
— Nia Donfris, 14

Twilight Zone Tower of Terror
Thrill Attraction : 2 to 3 Minutes : Must be 40 Inches Tall

The tallest structure on Disney World property is home to one of its most thrilling attractions: the Twilight Zone Tower of Terror. On this attraction, you endure one of our biggest fears in humans—an elevator that has gone off the track and is out of control. In this case, the elevator has become haunted on the 13th floor and takes you on a series of rises, dips, finally a long fall to the floor as the attraction comes to the end.

Most Disney thrill attractions have a "chicken out" exit for guests who get scared when they get to the head of the line. In this attraction's case, the "chicken out" exit is an elevator ride to the ground floor.

Like Rock 'n' Roller Coaster, this is a very popular attraction and will have queues that get longer and longer as the day goes on. FastPass+ reservations are available and highly recommended.

Educational Slant: Why are people afraid of falling in an elevator? What causes phobias/fears in people? What can be done to help people overcome their fears?

Disney's Tower of Terror has a random number of drops, making each ride different.
— Ben Bratton, 12

I like going on Tower of Terror by myself. I will stare blankly at everyone and join in the fun.
— Julia Abrams, 16

CHAPTER FIVE

Animal Kingdom

THE OASIS

The Oasis Exhibits

Walkthrough Attraction : Your Own
Pace: No Height Restriction

The Oasis is one of six themed areas in Animal Kingdom. It's two things in one. First, it is the area where Guest Relations and other services are located. This is where you can pick up park maps, and pick up and drop off strollers, if you have small children in your party. Second, the wide variety of Oasis animal exhibits are located on the walk back into the rest of the park.

There are a variety of habitats for the different types of animals. You'll see exotic birds like the Australian White Ibis, Ruddy Ducks, and Hyacinth Macaws. Animals are also present on these trails, including Giant Anteaters, Florida Cooters (a type of turtle), and Swamp Wallabies.

There are areas when you can take pictures of the animals and birds. There is more information about them in each area where you can learn about their habitat and behavior.

Educational Slant: What makes an animal decide on what environment is best for it to live in? If the animal was placed in a new environment, not Disney World, would be able to survive? What adaptations, if any, would it need to make?

DISCOVERY ISLAND

It's Tough to be a Bug

Show Attraction (4D show—glasses required)
: 9 minutes long: No Height Restriction

This attraction is loosely based on the movie of the same name. Flik, the main character from the movie, takes you on a journey into the insect kingdom and attempts to educate you on why insects should be viewed as helpful and not harmful. 3D glasses are required for this show.

This attraction is located completely inside the Tree of Life, Animal Kingdom's iconic symbol. A variety of insects are introduced to the audience, from stinkbugs to spiders to beetles to weevils. You learn about what makes these insects tick and the benefits they can provide to the environment. There is one scary scene where the black widow attempts to capture the audience so those who are easily scared, be warned. There is also a scene where the stinkbug "gasses" the audience, adding to the "4D" effects of the show.

Educational Slant: Pick a type of insect from the show and research it. Learn where it comes from, where it likes to live, where it likes to hide, who are its predators, and what are its defense mechanisms.

Discovery Island Trails

Walkthrough Attraction: At Your Own
Pace: No Height Restriction

Very similar to The Oasis Exhibits. You have the opportunity to view more animals in their habitats. These trails wind through and around the Tree of Life.

The Tree of Life can viewed as an attraction all on its own. The tree has over 300 animal carvings in its bark. Sometimes along these trails and near the Tree of Life you'll catch sight of a character known as DiVine. She hides in the flora and fauna of the Discovery Island Trails and other parts of Animal Kingdom. Most of the time, guests do not know she is there until she brushes you with one of her branches. So be on the lookout!

The two long pathways of the Discovery Island Trails lead you on a self-guided tour through a variety of exotic habitats and animals, including otters, kangaroos, tortoises, storks, and lemurs. Disney cast members knowledgeable about the animals also roam the trails and can answer your questions.

Educational Slant: Research conservation efforts in the different regions of the world where the animals come from. Research an animal and its environment. Research camouflage and how both animals and DiVine use camouflage to go unseen.

Wilderness Explorers

Through All of Animal Kingdom : At Your
Own Pace : No Height Restriction

This attraction is inspired by Doug from the movie *UP* and his inquisitive nature as a Wilderness Explorer scout. It has locations throughout the park where you can sign up to become a Wilderness Explorer. The first location is in Discovery Island. As you travel through the park, you'll participate in different activities and earn badges to fill up your guidebook.

Since this attraction requires a lot of walking and a lot of tasks, do not be surprised if you can't complete all of the tasks in one visit. There is a lot to see and do within Animal Kingdom, but these Wilderness Explorer locations provide learning experiences that you can share with your classmates when you return to school.

Educational Slant: This attraction is all about education. You earn different types of badges that vary from learning how to play an African drum to the health of sea turtles to simply finding different types of animals within the park. These are great things for kids both young and old to explore and earn badges, all while learning about animals and different cultures.

AFRICA

Festival of the Lion King

Show Attraction : 30 minutes : No Height Restriction

This is one of the best shows at Disney World. It is also one of the most popular attractions within Animal Kingdom. Shows takes place on the hour. You have two ways to get in: use a FastPass+ reservation or stand in line. Guests who use a FastPass+ reservation are asked to arrive 30 minutes before their show begins. Guests who do not use FastPass+ should either attend one of the morning shows or be prepared to wait. The theater is big so most people in the stand-by line get in, but it is not guaranteed.

Once inside, the 30 minutes fly by. Guests are sectioned off into four cheering sections for an experience that is part stage show and part circus, with music from *The Lion King* played throughout. There is a lot of singing and dancing. You will have the songs stuck in your head for most of the day after watching the show. It is a must-see attraction at Animal Kingdom.

Educational Slant: You can move away from animals and botany for this attraction. Spend time learning more about the different rhythm and music patterns used in the show. Write about ways the different leaders of the cheering sections motivated their section to cheer louder and win the competition. Research the skills it takes to be an acrobat.

Kilimanjaro Safari

Ride Attraction : 22 Minutes : No Height Restriction

Another must-do attraction at Animal Kingdom, Kilimanjaro Safari is one of the largest safari rides in the world, covering almost 5,000,000 square feet. It is also a FastPass+ eligible ride. I recommend that you and your party get FastPass+ reservations unless you arrive early in the morning. Wait times in the morning are low as cast members are able to load people on the 32-passenger vehicles quickly. As the day goes on, the wait times get longer, then drop later in the afternoon and early evening. However, you are likely to see fewer animals during these times as more of them are feeding or asleep. Definitely, a morning attraction.

You'll see lots of animals on the Kilimanjaro Safari, and you can take as many pictures as you please provided that your body remains within the frame of the open-air ride vehicle. One of my best tips for this attractions is to have one person act as the "spotter" for the photographer. Look ahead on the trail for animals so the photographer can be ready. You'll encounter lions, cheetahs, hippos, crocodiles, flamingos, gazelles, rhinos, and other animals along this 22-minute ride through the savannah.

Educational Slant: This is a great attraction to learn about a wide variety of African animals and their habitats. After you return home, research these habitats and examine if they're under threat of poachers and what the local people are doing to protect the animals from these threats.

Pangani Forest Exploration Trail

Walkthrough Attraction : At Your Own Pace : No Height Restriction

The Pangani Forest Exploration Trail, like the Oasis Exhibits and the Discovery Island Trails, is another walk-through animal attraction. This trail focuses solely on

African animals and can be found near the exit to the Kilimanjaro Safari.

The trail starts with the monkey exhibit and winds through the forest visiting a cross-section of the different types of animals that live in Africa. Some of the animals don't mind having their picture taken, while others are private and will run away from people or only come out a night. Maybe when Avatarland debuts and Animal Kingdom is open later into the evening, you'll have a better chance of seeing the animals that are more nocturnal in nature.

The trails ends with the gorilla exhibit and its two viewing areas: one where you can view the gorillas behind glass, the other an open-air viewing area. In both areas, you're asked to be as quiet as possible so the gorillas are not scared into hiding. A good tour of the trail should take around 30 minutes.

Educational Slant: Compare the animals that you see on the trail to the animals that you saw on Kilimanjaro Safari. Are there any similarities or differences in their behaviors? What can cause an animal to be scared or feel threatened?

Wildlife Express Train

Train Ride : 7 Minutes : No Height Restriction

This train ride takes guests from the Africa on a 1.2 mile journey to Rafiki's Planet Watch. You get to see what makes Animal Kingdom tick as you ride past some of the medical facilities for the animals as well as the housing for the rhinos and elephants.

Rafiki's Planet Watch is a region of the park devoted to learning in-depth about the animals seen in the parks and in the wilds of Florida. When you're done at Rafiki's Planet Watch, you hop back on the train for the 1.2 mile trip back to Africa and the rest of Animal Kingdom.

Why a train ride? Walt Disney loved trains and 1.2 miles is a long way to walk to a region of the park.

Educational Slant: How are the veterinarians helping the animals? What does it take to become a veterinarian? Is it easier or harder than becoming a doctor?

RAFIKI'S PLANET WATCH

Rafiki's Planet Watch is a region of the park only accessible by train. It's devoted to the preservation and conservation of animal habitats, and has three sections.

Habitat Habit

Walkthrough Attraction : At Your Own Pace : No Height Restriction

It is very hard to call Habitat Habit an attraction even though it is listed as one on the Animal Kingdom map. It's really just a bunch of plaques with information about animal habitats on them as you walk from the train station to the inner workings of Rafiki's Planet Watch. There is very little to see outside of these plaques. There will be very little to no animal interaction.

Conservation Station

Walkthrough Attraction : At Your Own Pace: No Height Restriction

Here you can learn about on-going conservation efforts in animal habitats throughout the world. There are a number of areas where you learn about different aspects of the conservation efforts. You can also explore veterinary medicine more in-depth in an area of the station geared toward how the animals are cared for. In another area, you can see how the animals interact with humans, while another is devoted to "spying on the animals" on hidden cameras throughout the Kilimanjaro Safari attraction. Lastly, there is an area where you can learn about how the animals are fed on a daily basis.

Educational slant: This attraction is all about education. Whether you are learning about conservation or veterinary medicine or nutrition, you are learning something in every section of the Conservation Station exhibit. Write about your experiences.

Affection Section
Walkthrough Attraction : At Your Own Pace : No Height Restriction

The Affection Section is the closest attraction that Disney has to a petting zoo. The animals here are the more "traditional" ones that most of you will see back home, including goats, pigs, cows, and sheep. You are allowed to go into the penned off areas to feed and/or pet the animals. Disney highly recommends that all guests who come in contact with the animals to wash their hands before and after entering the penned off area. This is to prevent the transmission of viruses and disease to the animals, and even more important, transmission to humans.

Educational Slant: Are any animals friendlier than others. What makes them so? Do they like to be brushed and fed? Is there anything that angers the animals?

ASIA

The Asia section of the park is home to four attractions: Flights of Wonder, Mahrajah Jungle Trek, Kali River Rapids, and Expedition Everest. This is the "thrill ride" section of Animal Kingdom. Mainly archecchiture from Southeast Asia can be found in this section of the park.

Flights of Wonder
Show Attraction : 25 Minutes : No Height Restriction

You are taken on journey, led by Guano Joe or Jane (depending on the show), through the wonders of exotic birds. During the 25-minute show, you will see up to 20 different exotic birds as they swoop and fly through the show area. Some of the birds are as small as a parrot, while others are as large as the Harris Hawk. These birds will delight you with their interactions with Guano Joe/Jane and will fly over the crowd as well.

This show is held outdoors with plenty of seating. No FastPass+ reservation are available. As an outdoor show, poor weather and storms can cancel the show or reduce it to a more educational show about the birds. Shows usually take place about once an hour during the day.

Educational slant: Write about the on-going conservation efforts for the habitats of the birds in the show. Do some research on a particular bird that interested you during the show. Compare the different flight patterns of the small birds and the larger birds. Plenty to learn and see here.

Mahrajah Jungle Trek

Walkthrough Attraction : At Your Own Pace : No Height Restriction

The Mahrajah Jungle Trek focuses on the animals of Asia. It is another walkthrough attraction where you can go at their own pace. There are lots of spots to take pictures of the animals along the trek. Try to take the pictures at the observation stations along the trek. It will keep the guests walking the trail behind you from walking into you and ruining your pictures. At the observation stations, information about the animals along the trek is displayed. Some of the animals that you will see along the trek are Asian tigers, blackbats, flying foxes, and over 50 species of birds.

Educational slant: Find an animal that interests you and learn about it (its habitat, conservation efforts to save it, etc.). You can also compare and contrast the Jungle Trek to the Pangani Forest Exploration Trail, and Discovery Island Trails (animals seen, length of trail, architecture, etc.).

Kali River Rapids

Thrill Attraction : 5 minutes : Guests
Must Be 38 Inches Tall to Ride

One of the few thrill attractions at Animal Kingdom, the Kali River Rapids is a trip down the Chakranadi River. There are 20 boats on the attraction and each boat can hold up to 12 guests. The queue is filled with artifacts from ancient ruins, temples, and fantastic landscaping. Once you get through the queue, your boat is waiting to take you on the five-minute trip down the river. The ride takes guests through an Asian forest and ends with a 30-foot drop down a waterfall. You *will* get wet on this attraction.

For guests that want to by-pass the queue, FastPass+ reservations are available, and going through the neighboring Jungle Trek is great way to pass the time while waiting for your FastPass+ to come up.

Educational Slant: Identify the different animal and bird calls. What does Disney Imagineering do to try to scare people on the attraction? Would the attraction be different if it were in the Africa section in the park? If so, how?

Expedition Everest

Thrill Attraction : 2 minutes 50 seconds :
Guests Must Be 44 Inches Tall to Ride

This is the most expensive roller coaster in the world. It cost Disney $100 million to build. The back story is that the Royal Anandapur Tea Company had many accidents along its train route by the infamous Yeti. As a result, they closed route. The locals have reconstructed the trail and take visitors around the base camp. There are two queues: the standard queue and the FastPass+/single rider line. The standard queue takes guests around the tourism company which the locals set up and then some Asian tea gardens. The other queue bypasses all of this interaction.

There are six train cars at Expedition Everest. However, only five of the cars are running at any given time. The highest drop on the attraction is 80 feet and the top speed is 50 miles per hour. The train takes guests around the base camp and then through a series of caves where you'll hear the Yeti's roar. At the end, the Yeti may or may not roar in an attempt to scare the guests.

Educational Slant: Research the Himalayan mountains? What makes them the highest mountains in the world.

A good spot to sit on Everest is if you want to go really, really fast is the back. But if you want to go slow you should probably sit in the front.
— Carter Witlse, 9

My favorite ride in the world is Expedition Everest. It goes backwards!
— Lucas Wilding, 10

DINOLAND USA

An homage to the traveling carnivals and 50s-style road-side attractions, DinoLand USA brings some dinosaur-themed carnival-style attractions to Animal Kingdom. Guests can also find a play land and a fossil adventure in this section of Animal Kingdom.

The Boneyard
Play land Attraction : At Your Own Pace: No Height Restriction

The younger set will be attracted to the Boneyard, a giant play land resembling an archaeological dig site. You can explore the large maze which winds through the attraction, dig for fossils, or drive a Jeep up and down the hills of the dig site. Parents: there is a shaded area with fans for you to rest while the kids are off exploring.

Educational slant: What is archaeology? What do you study? Is it a field of study that you may be interested in?

Fossil FunGames

Carnival-style Games : At Your Own Pace : No Height Restriction

Fossil Fun Games brings the carnival atmosphere to DinoLand USA. These games of chance are seen through-out DinoLand. They are just like the games you see at local traveling carnivals and include:

- Whac-A-Packycephalosaur
- Fossil Fueler
- Mammoth Marathon
- Comet Crasher
- Bronto-Score

The cost of these games is not covered under your admission to Animal Kingdom. You can use your MagicBand to pay for them. Prizes include Disney-themed stuffed animals.

Educational Slant: Learn about the psychology of getting people to play carnival games: what do the game host/carnival barkers say to entice people to play? What sounds to the games themselves make to attract people?

Finding Nemo—The Musical

Show Attraction : 40 Minutes : No Height Restriction

Taking place in Disney's Theater of the Wild is Finding Nemo—The Musical. Like Festival of the Lion King, Finding Nemo is one of Disney's best show attractions. It takes place several times a day (usually on the hour). This attraction also takes FastPass+ reservations; you're asked to arrive 30 minutes in advance to gain entry into the show. You can also wait in the stand-by line, but doing so does not mean you will gain access to the next showing. Best strategy is to see an early showing or make a FastPass+ reservation.

Once in the theater, you're transported under the ocean to see a stage re-enactment of the movie *Finding Nemo*. Scenes and songs from the movie are present through the show. One of the best parts is how the cast members use puppetry to bring the scenes to life. Full of lively songs and great stage presentation, the entire family will enjoy Finding Nemo—The Musical

Educational Slant: Learn more about puppetry and how puppets can bring a show to life with the right puppet master. Listen to the music from the show; how does it bring the viewer into the show? Does it complement the stage performance? What other ways can music help a stage performance?

Primeval Whirl

Thrill Attraction : 1 Minute 30 Seconds :
Must be 48 Inches Tall

Primeval Whirl is a "wild mouse" style of roller coaster. A wild-mouse roller coaster is one that has small cars (four people or less) and has really sharp turns with very little or no banking. There are short transition areas before heading into another section of sharp turns and switchbacks (180-degree turns). Taller riders could experience the sensation of whiplash because their heads are exposed from the car while smaller riders have the seat pads to cushion their heads from the extreme nature of the turns.

Primeval Whirl takes its cue from this style of ride. The dinosaur-themed attraction is a short ride at only 1 minute 30 seconds. Guests are taken back to the primeval era as the car spins its way to the top of the roller coaster. As you work your way back to the bottom and the present, the car will spin and take wild turns back and forth.

This attraction accept FastPass+ reservations. Wait times are never really long compared to other thrill rides at Animal Kingdom. Save one of your reservations for a busier attraction.

Educational Slant: Research what makes a wild-mouse roller coaster different from a traditional roller coaster. What is whiplash? Are there long-term effects from experiencing whiplash?

Triceratop Spin

Spinner Attraction : 1 Minute 30 Seconds : No Height Restriction

Triceratop Spin is a dinosaur-themed spinner attraction based off the Dumbo attraction in Magic Kingdom. Like Primeval Whirl, it is a short ride at only 1 minute and 30 seconds. There are around 15 dinosaur vehicles that spin around a center post. Each dinosaur has a front row of seats and a back row. Each row has its own set of controls for the dinosaur during the ride. The front row controls the pitch (whether it is nose down or nose up), and the back row controls how high the dinosaur is flying. The ride ends with all of the dinosaurs going as high as they can before being lowered to the staging area.

Educational Slant: This is a great attraction to learn about flying. How does lift help something fly in the air? What happens what something dives down? Do they lift to "pull out of the dive"? How does the wheel-and-spoke mechanism of the attraction work?

DINOSAUR

Thrill Attraction : 3 minutes 30 Seconds : Must be 40 Inches Tall

This attraction is part track ride, part motion simulator. You get in a car and travel back in time with the quest of retrieving a dinosaur before the species goes extinct. When you arrive in the past, there is an asteroid about to impact the Earth. The car moves around larger dinosaurs which roar and try to attack the car. In the end, the car leaves prehistoric Earth with its dinosaur in tow and comes back to the present. The attraction is very dark and has lots of roaring dinosaurs which will scare youngsters.

DINOSAUR is a continuous loading attraction. This means it can put a lot of people through in a short period of time. As a result, the wait times are not long (though the wait does build as the day goes on). FastPass+ reservations are available. Use your three FastPass+ attractions on other attractions and then your fourth FastPass+ (which you gain access to after using the first three) on DINOSAUR.

Educational Slant: Research the time when the asteroid hit the Earth: where did it impact? What happened when it did? What caused the dinosaurs to go extinct? Could humans and dinosaurs have co-existed?

CHAPTER SIX

Dining

The Disney Dining Plan can be overwhelming upon first glance. There are lots of food options. Lots of different categories for meals. Will I be able to use all of my credits? And so on. Parents: I have included the pricing for the different levels of dining plans. This is a great opportunity to sit down with your children and show them budgeting for a vacation and comparing different plans to each other.

There are three categories of food at Disney World: snack, quick-service meal, and table-service meal:

- A snack is something that can be purchased at either a snack cart or a quick-service restaurant. Examples of snacks are a 20 oz. bottle of soda or water, a scoop of popcorn, 12 oz. coffee, or a bag of pre-packaged snacks. Typically, if it costs under $5, it counts as a Disney snack.

- A quick-service meal is one in which you go up to the counter, order your food, and wait for it there. The only exception to this is Be Our Guest where for easier queue management you order your food from an electronic kiosk and then go to find a table. A cast member will bring the food to your table.

- A table-service meal is like going out to eat at a restaurant. You're seated at the table, menus are brought to you, and you're waited on by a cast member.

Disney allocates the number of snacks, quick-service meals, and table-service meals based on the number of NIGHTS in a stay. For example, each member in a family on a four-night stay and on the standard dining plan will get 4 snacks, 4 quick-service meals, and 4 table-service meals. A couple of years ago, Disney also included the price of a refillable mug in the dining plan, so each family member will get one of those, too.

When you add the Disney Dining Plan to your resort stay (guests staying off-property cannot take advantage of the dining plan), you have three packages to choose from: quick-service, standard, and deluxe. Here's a breakdown of what's included in all three packages.

- Quick-service dining (per person): 2 quick-service meals (per night), 1 snack (per night), 1 refillable mug (per stay). No table-service credits are included. The cost per night of this package is $44.13 for guests aged 10 and up; $19.04 for guests aged 3 through 9.

- Standard dining (per person): 1 quick-service meal (per night), 1 snack (per night), 1 table-service meal (per night), 1 refillable mug (per stay). The cost per night of this package is $63.70 for guests aged 10 and up; $22.85 for guests aged 3 through 9.

- Deluxe dining (per person): 3 counter or table-service meals (per night), 2 snacks (per night), 1 refillable mug (per stay). The cost per night of this dining package is $115.08 for guests aged 10 and up; $35.49 for guests 3 through 9.

Gratuity is NOT included in the cost of the table-service meals under the standard and deluxe dining plan. This comes "out of pocket" and can be charged back to the room.

At the end of every quick or table meal, you will get a receipt that shows how many credits are remaining on your plan.

For snacks and quick-service meals, there is no distinction between "adult" snacks and "child" snacks. They are all lumped together. For table-service meals, however, they do make the distinction, and the credits are broken down into adult table-service credits remaining and child table-service credits remaining.

One Credit and Two Credit Table-Service Meals

Most table-service meals cost one credit, but some (due to their cost and/or popularity) cost two. They are: Jiko—The Cooking Place (Animal Kingdom Lodge), Flying Fish Cafe (Boardwalk), California Grill (Contemporary), Citricos and Narcoossee's (Grand Floridan), Artist Point (Wilderness Lodge), Yachtsman Steakhouse (Yacht and Beach Clubs), Le Cellier (Canada Pavilion in Epcot), Monsieur Paul (France Pavilion in Epcot), Hollywood Brown Derby (Hollywood Studios), Fulton's Crab House and the Dining Room at Wolfgang Puck's Grand Cafe (Disney Springs).

In addition, Fairytale Dining at Cinderella's Royal Table, Hoop-Dee-Doo Musical Revue, Mickey's Backyard BBQ, and Spirit of Aloha Dinner Show cost two credits, as do all room-service meals and pizza deliveries.

Making Table-Service Reservations

Disney strongly recommends making reservations for all table-service meals. You can start making reservations at 180 days from the start of your vacation. Does it seem odd to know what you are going to eat on vacation but not know what you are going to eat next Tuesday? Yes, it does. But this planning is necessary. Reservations, for some restaurants, fill up quickly.

The best plan of attack is to use the table reservations as your day-by-day planning guide for the parks. This is what my family does. If we have an evening table-service reservation at Hollywood Studios, we may choose to go to another park in the morning. Then, we return to our room after lunch and recharge by the pool in the afternoon before heading to Hollywood Studios riding an attraction or two before our dinner reservation. The opposite would hold true for a morning table-service reservation.

But overall, my best advice for making dining reservations is to make them right on the 180-day mark. Reservations can be made starting at 6 a.m. Eastern (online) and 7 a.m. Eastern via the phone. This provides you with the best chance of getting the reservations you want at the time you want them. Have a prioritized list of restaurants ready to go when making reservations, with back-ups in case your first picks fail.

Toughest-to-Get Dining Reservations

- Cinderella's Royal Table
- Be Our Guest
- Akershus Royal Banquet Hall
- Chef Mickey
- Le Cellier
- Victoria and Albert's
- Any of the dinner shows (Hoop Dee Doo Revue, Spirit of Aloha Dinner Show)

For the character meals (Cinderella's Royal Table, Akershus Royal Banquet Hall, and Chef Mickey's), great back-up choices are 1900 Park Fare at Grand Floridian, Tusker House in Animal Kingdom, and 'Ohana at the Polynesian. For Le Cellier, an excellent back-up is Yachtsman Steakhouse at the Yacht Club while a Trail's End dinner is good substitute for the Hoop Dee Doo Musical Revue.

Easier-to-Get Dining Reservations

- Any of the moderate resort table-service restaurants (Maya Grille, Shutters, etc.)
- Biergarten in the Germany Pavilion at Epcot

- Plaza Restaurant in the Magic Kingdom
- Tony's Town Square in the Magic Kingdom
- Wave of American Flavors in the Contemporary
- The Grand Floridian Café at the Grand Floridian

Plan your dining reservations as a family. Depending on the size of the family or length of the vacation, put each person is in charge of one or more days of dining. This helps give everyone in the family "ownership" in the vacation because they have invested time and effort in selecting a restaurant.

Disney World offers many quick-service to grab a quick bite to eat while in a park or at a resort. There are too many to list in this book, but check out the Disney World website itself, which lists every restaurant (quick and table) on property, and provides current menus for most.

Dinner Shows

Restaurant: Hoop Dee Doo Musical Revue
Location: Fort Wilderness
Meals Available: Dinner Only
Cost: Adults $$$$, Kids $$, Disney Dining Plan: two table-service credits per person

This is the only dinner show was takes place inside and you get a fun Western-style meal. The main dishes are fried chicken, mashed potatoes, and strawberry shortcake for dessert. There is plenty of slapstick-style comedy in between and during the musical numbers.

Restaurant: Mickey's Backyard BBQ
Location: Fort Wilderness
Meals Available: Dinner Only
Cost: Adults $$$$, Kids $$, Disney Dining Plan: two table-service credits per person

This dinner show takes place in an open-air pavilion (versus the air-conditioned comfort of Hoop Dee Doo).

If you are looking for characters at the dinner show, then this is the show for you. Mickey's Backyard BBQ is the only dinner show with character interaction. The food is pretty straightforward, with plenty of BBQ on the menu (ribs, chicken), corn on the cob, etc.

Allow plenty of travel time to both Hoop Dee Doo and Mickey's Backyard BBQ. There is no bus from the resorts to Fort Wilderness. You'll need to get a bus from your resort to the Magic Kingdom and then take a boat to Fort Wilderness OR go to a theme park and take a bus directly there.

Restaurant: Spirit of Aloha Dinner Show
Location: Polynesian Village Resort
Meals Available: Dinner Only
Cost: Adults $$$$, Kids $$, Disney Dining Plan: two table-service credits per person

A Polynesian luau in Florida is the basis for the Spirit of Aloha Dinner Show. It's the best of the three dinner shows with lots of entertainment up on the stage while you enjoy the show in covered outdoor seating. The food has a Polynesian flair with lots of pork and chicken on the menu while still serving standard fare for the kids, including chicken nuggets and macaroni and cheese.

CHAPTER SEVEN

Dining Plan

This chapter looks at one of the most difficult questions to answer about a Disney World vacation. Do I get the Disney Dining Plan, purchase a Tables in Wonderland card (if I am a Disney annual passholder, Disney Vacation Club (DVC) member, or a Florida resident), or do I just pay out-of-pocket?

- The Disney Dining Plan is the pre-paid options. It allows you to pay for your food up front as part of your vacation package. (See the previous chapters for details.) A "meal", under the dining plan, is an entrée and non-alcoholic beverage for break-fast, and an entrée, a dessert, and a non-alcoholic beverage for lunch and dinner. Buffets come with a non-alcoholic beverage, as well.

- Tables in Wonderland is a card available to annual passholders, Florida residents, and DVC members. The card offers a discount (usually 20%) at select table-service restaurants. When using the card, the bill automatically adds an 18% gratuity to the bill. The card is subject to blackout dates. The cost is $100 for annual passholders and DVC members and $125 for Florida residents. It's good for one year from date of purchase.

- Paying out of pocket means you pay for all your meals and snacks like you would at home. You open your wallet and pay face value for the food.

Which method is the best? That depends completely on your family's eating habits. Sit down and do a cost comparison of the three methods and see which one is best. *Paying out-of-pocket is almost always the worst option, so it* will usually come down to the Disney Dining Plan or Tables in Wonderland.

Let's plan a hypothetical six-night stay at Disney World (two adults/one child):

Table-Service Meals

We'll assume three true table-service meals and three character meals just so the kids aren't expecting a character to appear at every meal. For ease of calculation, the two adults order the exact same meal.

- Chef Mickey's for dinner: $45.79/adult, $22.89/ child
- Via Napoli for dinner: $26.00 (chicken parm) + $10.00 (zeppol di caternia) + $3.00 (beverage); children's meal $9.50
- Cape May Cafe for breakfast: $28.75/adult; $15.44/ child
- Chefs des France (note Chefs des France does not have a TiW discount but does have a 10% DVC discount): Prix Fixe Menu $39.99 + $3.00 (beverage); children's meal $9.50
- 1900 Park Fare for dinner: $41.42/adult; $20.23/ child
- Mama Melrose for lunch: $32.99 (strip steak)+$8.00 (dessert)+$3.00 (beverage); children's meal $8.50

Quick-Service Meals

- ABC Commissary: $9.59 (chicken club sandwich) + $4.19 (chocolate mousse) + $3.00 (beverage); children's meal $6.00

- Be Our Guest: $12.99 (braised pork) + $4.19 (cup-cake) + $3.00 (beverage); children's meal $8.50
- Contempo Cafe: $10.19 (Italian Sandwich) + 4.69 (cupcake) + $3.00 (beverage); children's meal $6.00
- Electric Umbrella: $10.99 (French Dip Burger) + $4.19 (cheesecake) + $3.00 (beverage); children's meal $6.00
- Flame Tree BBQ: $10.99 (1/2 BBQ chicken) + $4.19 (Key Lime Mousse) + $3.00 (beverage); children's meal $6.00
- Gaston's Tavern: $9.79 (pork shank) + $3.29 (crois-sant) + $3.00 (beverage); purchase child's meal at Casey's $8.29 (hot dog meal)

Snacks *(each guest gets the same snacks)*

- Scoop of Popcorn $3.50
- Scoop of Popcorn $3.50
- Mickey Ice Cream Bar $4.00
- Contempo Cupcake $4.69
- Churro $4.00
- Scoop of Ice Cream from L'Artisan des Glace $4.00

Let's tally up the totals (Tables in Wonderland includes the cost of the card):

Per Adult
- Disney Dining Plan: $360.24
- Tables In Wonderland: $328.52
- Out of Pocket: $371.92

Per Child
- Disney Dining Plan: $115.38
- Tables In Wonderland: $134.26
- Out of Pocket: $150.26

For an adult, Tables in Wonderland is the best deal. For children, however, the best deal is the Disney Dining Plan. Let's see what happens when we merge our family of three (two adults/one Disney child):

- Disney Dining Plan: $835.36
- Tables In Wonderland: $891.30
- Out of Pocket: $894.36

Tables in Wonderland is the best deal for just the food. However, the $100 cost of the card has to be factored in and that pushes the total to almost the same amount as paying out of pocket.

Now let's see what happens when the child turns 10 and becomes a "Disney adult". When a guest pays cash or charges a meal back to the room, the age restriction on the children's menu goes away. Anybody can order off the kids' menu. For buffet meals, though, anyone over 10 gets charged as an adult.

This brings our totals to:

- Disney Dining Plan: $1,091.52
- Tables In Wonderland: $937.24
- Out of Pocket: $951.78

Tables in Wonderland still works out to be a slightly better deal on our hypothetical vacation. This just accounts for the food, not the gratuity. And again, your numbers based on your vacation may vary. It's best to sit down and try to plan out your meals ahead of time and see which situation works best for you.

CHAPTER EIGHT

Dining: Character Meals

Disney World provides many opportunities to have a meal with the characters. These meals take place in both the theme parks and at some of the resorts. Why wait in the sun when you sit in the comfort of air conditioning and have the characters come to you?

Character meal dining requires a dining reservation which can be made 180 days in advance either on the Disney World website or by calling 407-939-DINE. When your vacation is 180 days away, you can start making reservations at 6 a.m. (Eastern) on the website and 7 a.m. (Eastern) via the phone. Kids, discuss with your parents what characters and meals that you would like to have while on your vacation, but save the actual making of the reservation to your parents.

In terms of cost, Disney allows children 2 and under to eat off an adult's plate for free (expect at buffets where they are given their own plate for sanitation purposes). Children aged 3–9 are considered kids. and if they are on the Disney Dining Plan, they are required to order off of the kids' menu. Children aged 10 and up are considered "Disney adults" and must order off the adult's menu if they are on the Disney Dining Plan. On occasion, a server may be nice and allow an older kid to order off the kids' menu, but it is not guaranteed.

With younger kids, I would make one character dining reservation for every "adult" dining reservation. This way, the kids are not expecting a character to appear at every meal. Remind them that on the "adult" dining reservations the characters will not be here as a way to manage expectations.

For older kids, you can be more selective on the number of character meals. If you are a returning vacationer, you can go to some old favorites or try new experiences. First-time visitors, find your favorite characters and seek out their dining experiences.

What to Expect at a Character Meal?

- Multiple characters: each table will have a chance to interact with every character that is part of the dining experience.

- Occasional singing and dancing: every 30–45 minutes, the characters will lead the diners in a sing-a-long. Kids are welcome to join the characters has they dance around the dining area.

- Usually a buffet or family-style dining: eat as much or as little as you like.

- Typical breakfast buffet items: Mickey-shaped waffles, omelettes, pancakes, bacon, sausage, hash browns/home fries, cereal, bagels, and fruit.

- Typical lunch and dinner buffet items: meat carving station (usually roast beef and turkey or ham), baked chicken, pasta, mashed potatoes, vegetables, salad. For the kids: Mickey-shaped mac and cheese and/or pasta, chicken nuggets, corn, broccoli, baked chicken.

- Typical desserts: soft-serve ice cream, brownies, assorted cakes and pies, cookies.

Animal Kingdom

Restaurant: Tusker House
Location: Africa
Meals with Characters: Breakfast, Lunch and Dinner
Characters: Donald Duck (host), Daisy Duck, Mickey Mouse, Goofy
Cost: Breakfast: adults $$, kids $; Lunch and Dinner: adults $$$, kids $; Disney Dining Plan: meal costs one table-service credit per person for breakfast, lunch, or dinner.

At this safari-style meal hosted by Donald Duck, food is served buffet-style with an African flair. Donald is joined by Daisy Duck, Mickey Mouse, and Goofy as they sing and dance their way around the restaurant. This is a fun meal, but it is not a dining reservation sought out by many guests who typically choose Chef Mickey's instead. One of the "easier" character meal reservations to obtain.

Epcot

Restaurant: The Garden Grill
Location: The Land Pavilion
Meals with Characters: Dinner Only
Characters: Chip n' Dale, Pluto, Mickey Mouse
Cost: Adults $$$, kids $; Disney Dining Plan: meal costs one table-service credit per person

This meal that takes you on a 360-degree journey over the Living with the Land greenhouses with hosts Chip n' Dale and appearances by Pluto and Mickey dressed in farmer attire. This is the easiest character dining reservation to get at Disney World. It's a great chance to have a long interaction with Mickey Mouse and not have a long wait to do so.

Restaurant: Akershus Royal Banquet Hall for Princess Storybook Dining
Location: Norway Pavilion
Meals with Characters: Breakfast, Lunch, and Dinner

Characters: Princesses appear on a rotating basis and may include Belle, Jasmine, Aurora, Snow White, Ariel (without fins), Cinderella, Mulan, or Mary Poppins

Costs: Breakfast: adults $$$ or $$$$, kids $$; Lunch: adults $$$ or $$$$, kids $$; Dinner: adults $$$$, kids: $$; Disney Dining Plan: meal costs one table-service credit per person

Norway hosts one of the most prized character dining reservations at Disney World: Princess Storybook Dining. The meals feature a rotating group of princesses. Typically, four or five princesses are a part of each meal, and this the only location where you can meet Ariel without her fins. Make your reservations as early as possible. The other unique feature of this character meal is that guests order from a menu. The food is not served buffet or family style.

Hollywood Studios

Restaurant: Hollywood and Vine (Play 'n' Dine)
Location: Echo Lake
Meals with Characters: Breakfast and Lunch
Characters: Disney Junior Characters (currently Sofia the First, Jake from *Jake and the Neverland Pirates*, and Doc McStuffins)
Costs: Breakfast: adults $$, kids $; lunch $$$, kids $; Disney Dining Plan: one table-service credit per person

Play 'n' Dine is the only location where you can have a meal with characters from the Disney Junior TV shows. It's one of the most light-hearted meals at Disney World with many opportunities for song and dance during your buffet-style meal. Lunch reservations are easy to come by, as a lot of people (presumably with smaller kids) opt for breakfast. Even with that in mind, the breakfast reservation is on the easier end of the scale to obtain.

A new character experience, at dinner, hosted by Minnie Mouse is now available. It has a seasonal theme and changes throughout the year.

Magic Kingdom

Restaurant: Crystal Palace
Location: Main Street, next to Adventureland entrance
Meals with Characters: Breakfast, Lunch, and Dinner
Characters: Winnie the Pooh, Tigger, Piglet, and Eeyore
Cost: Breakfast: adults $$, kids $; Lunch: adults $$ or $$$, kids $; Dinner $$$ kids $; Disney Dining Plan: one table-service credit per person

Jump into the Hundred Acre Wood with Winnie the Pooh and Friends and enjoy a fun-filled meal. It's Friend's Day at Crystal Palace and Winnie the Pooh and his pals make sure that they make lots of new friends during this dining experience. Every 30 to 60 minutes, you get to join in singing the "Friendship Song" as the kids dance around the dining room with Winnie the Pooh. This is a difficult reservation to get, especially for breakfast which starts at 8 a.m., before the Magic Kingdom opens (except on days with Extra Magic Hours) so you can experience an empty park and if you finish your meal quickly can get to the front of the line for popular Magic Kingdom attractions or character meet and greets.

> *I like Crystal Palace because they such a variety of options and I love the triangle cinnamon toast. My mom even makes it at home for me.*
> — Corbin Wiltse, 11

Restaurant: Cinderella's Royal Table
Location: The Hub (center of Magic Kingdom)
Meals with Characters: Breakfast, Lunch, and Dinner
Characters: Cinderella, The Fairy Godmother, Gus Gus, Jacques (dinner), Snow White, Belle, and Jasmine (breakfast and lunch)
Cost: Breakfast: adults $$$$, kids $$$; Lunch: adults $$$$, kids $$$, Dinner—adults $$$$, kids $$$; Disney Dining Plan: two table-service credits per person

This is THE most difficult reservation to get at Disney World because it is a chance to dine inside Cinderella Castle. You're greeted when you arrive by Cinderella (at lunch and dinner) and the Fairy Godmother (at dinner) who pose for a picture which is included in the cost of your reservation. Each child on the reservation will receive a special gift (usually a fairy wand for the girls and a pirate sword for the boys). Like dining in Norway, guests order off a menu. There is no dancing with the characters here, though if you are lucky, you may get to see the Prince dance with Cinderella.

For beginners I would start at Cinderella Castle to eat because it's a good experience if you're a first timer, second timer or third timer.
— Carter Wiltse, 9

Character Meals at the Resorts

Restaurant: Cape May Café
Location: Beach Club
Meals with Characters: Breakfast Only
Characters: Goofy, Donald, and Minnie
Cost: Adults $$, Kids $; Disney Dining Plan: one table-service credit per person

Goofy is joined only by Donald and Minnie, but what is lacking in number of characters is more than made up or in character interactions. The characters have plenty of time to move from table to table to interact with guests. I ate here, a few years ago, and one of the members of our party had excused themselves to the washroom. She returned to find Donald sitting in her seat with a napkin over his eyes taking a nap until she returned! Reservations are easy to come by given the small number of characters. Beach Club has a great location between Epcot and Hollywood Studios which makes the breakfast a great start to your day before heading to either park.

My favorite restaurant is Cape May at the Beach Club Resort at dinner. I love their crab legs and their raspberry fudge dessert is delicious! - Hannah McDaniel, 12

Restaurant: Chef Mickey's
Location: The Contemporary (4th floor)
Meals with Characters: Breakfast, Brunch, and Dinner
Characters: Mickey, Minnie, Donald Duck, Goofy, and Pluto
Cost: Breakfast: adults $$ or $$$, kids $ or $$; Brunch—adults $$$, kids $$; Dinner $$$ or $$$$, kids $$; Disney Dining Plan: one table-service credit per person

Join in the singing and dancing while having a napkin-waving good time at Chef Mickey's inside the Contemporary. You start your meal with a photo in front of Chef Mickey which is included in the cost of the reservation. From there, you enjoy a fabulous buffet and in a great location where you can wave to the monorail on its way to the Magic Kingdom or enjoy a view of Seven Seas Lagoon. This is a great place to meet the "Big Five" Disney characters which will allow you to spend time in the parks on attractions as opposed to waiting in line to meet characters. The food is excellent and the fun is non-stop.

Restaurant: 1900 Park Fare
Location: Grand Floridian
Meals with Characters: Breakfast (Supercalifragilistic Breakfast) and Dinner (Cinderella's Happily Ever After Dinner)
Characters: Breakfast—Mary Poppins, Alice, The Mad Hatter; Dinner—Cinderella, Prince Charming, Fairy Godmother, Lady Tremaine, Evil Step Sisters (Anastasia and Drizella)
Cost: Breakfast: adults $$ kids $; Dinner: adults $$$ kids $

If you're looking for a great "fallback" restaurant if you can't get that Cinderella's Royal Table reservation, then look no further than 1900 Park Fare which provides two completely different character experiences at lunch and dinner. Both meals have great character interaction, especially the Evil Step Sisters who will fight over the boys in attendance to be their suitors. The Grand Floridian is a great location only a short boat or monorail ride from Magic Kingdom, making it an ideal place to start or end a day at that park.

I got to dress up and eat a buffet. I love buffets! And the stepsisters were really funny, too!
— Morgan Pouncey, 9

Interacting with the characters is my favorite part of dinner. We always try to throw something new at them every time we visit. The food is really good, especially the strawberry soup and mini cannolis!
— Kate Nicely, 10

Restaurant: 'Ohana
Location: Polynesian Village Resort
Meals With Characters: Breakfast Only
Characters: Lilo, Stitch, Mickey, and Pluto
Cost: Adults $$, Kids $; Disney Dining Plan: One table-service credit per person

Aloha and welcome to 'Ohana's Best Friends Breakfast featuring Lilo and Stitch. You'll enjoy a family-style meal which is brought right to your table. Younger children will enjoy singing and dancing with the characters as they make their way around the dining room. The food is excellent and includes all the Mickey-shaped waffles you can eat. Another restaurant with a great location to start a Magic Kingdom day.

CHAPTER NINE

Dining: Non-Character Meals

Disney World has many options for non-character meals. Every theme park has many table-service restaurants; Epcot, given its vast size, has the most. Every deluxe and most moderate resorts have at least one such restaurant.

Animal Kingdom

Restaurant: Rainforest Cafe
Location: Just outside Animal Kingdom
Meals Available: Breakfast, Lunch, and Dinner
Cost: Adults $$, Kids $, Disney Dining Plan: one table-service credit per person

Located just outside Animal Kingdom, Rainforest Café provides diners a unique dining experience inside a rainforest environment. Enjoy tropical-infused cuisine while hearing the callings of birds and animals from deep inside the rainforest. You can order the popular Tonga Toast at breakfast.

Restaurant: Yak and Yeti
Location: Asia
Meals Available: Lunch and Dinner
Cost: Adults $$, Kids $, Disney Dining Plan: one table-service credit per person

Head into the mountains of Nepal to the Yak and Yeti restaurant for Pan-Asian cuisine. A great place to take a mid-day break or end your day at Animal Kingdom.

Epcot

Restaurant: Chefs de France
Location: France Pavilion
Meals Available: Lunch and Dinner
Cost: Adults $$, Kids $, Disney Dining Plan: one table-service credit per person

Enjoy some of the best French cuisine at Disney World at Chefs de France. You'll be able to take a tour of French cuisine while watching other guests hustling and bustling through the World Showcase. Remy used to make appearance during dinner, but has not been seen in a long time.

Restaurant: Coral Reef
Location: The Seas Pavilion
Meals Available: Lunch and Dinner
Cost: Adults $$, Kids $, Disney Dining Plan: one table-service credit per person

Guests dine "under the sea" and experience a meal next to one of the giant aquariums that make up the Seas Pavilion at Epcot. Seafood is the primary item on the menu, but there is just enough beef and chicken items to keep the "carnivores" in the family happy.

Restaurant: La Hacienda de San Angel
Location: Mexico Pavilion
Meals Available: Dinner Only
Cost: Adults $$, Kids $, Disney Dining Plan: one table-service credit per person

Located on the World Showcase Lagoon, La Hacienda de San Angel provides a taste of Mexico in a fun and open-air restaurant. You'll enjoy great food and, if you get there late enough, an excellent view of Illuminations from inside.

Restaurant: Le Cellier
Location: Canada Pavilion
Meals Available: Lunch and Dinner
Cost: Adults $$$, Kids $, Disney Dining Plan: two table-service credits per person

Le Cellier, in French, means the Cellar. You're taken into a Canadian wine cellar to enjoy some of the best that Canada has to offer. The marquee items are the steak dishes along with the cheddar cheese soup, a Le Cellier specialty. The restaurant does not have a large footprint, so reservations are hard to come by and the tables are very close together.

Restaurant: Monsieur Paul
Location: France Pavilion
Meals Available: Dinner Only
Cost: Adults $$$$, Kids $$, Disney Dining Plan: two table-service credits per person

Monsieur Paul, located above Chefs de France, is a very intimate dining experience with views of the World Showcase. The menu is created by Chef Francisco Santin on a continuous basis using the best and freshest foods that France has to offer. Reservations for this dining experience are difficult to obtain.

> *My favorite snacks are the chocolate macarons*
> *at L'artisan des Glaces in France at Epcot.*
> — Hannah McDaniel, 12

Restaurant: Nine Dragons
Location: China Pavilion
Meals Available: Lunch and Dinner
Cost: Adults $$, Kids $, Disney Dining Plan: one table-service credit per person

Take a tour of Chinese cuisine at Nine Dragons. The menu features food from across the vast country of China. You'll be able to enjoy both the spice and the sweet in the dishes.

Restaurant: Restaurant Marrakesh
Location: Morocco Pavilion
Meals Available: Dinner Only
Cost: Adults $$, Kids $, Disney Dining Plan: one table-service credit per person

Travel to northern Africa and visit Restaurant Marrakesh where you can enjoy lamb, shish kebab, and couscous while belly dancers sway to the rhythms of North Africa. Don't fear picky eaters; there is some traditional fare on the menu (mainly the kids' menu).

Restaurant: Rose and Crown Pub and Dining Room
Location: United Kingdom Pavilion
Meals Available: Lunch and Dinner
Cost: Adults $$, Kids $, Disney Dining Plan: one table-service credit per person

It's named the Rose and Crown as those words appear most frequently in English pubs. You can enjoy a taste of the United Kingdom at Epcot. Meat pies, bangers and mash, and fish and chips feature prominently on the menu. For the less food adventurous, there is a grilled steak and grilled chicken. Another great spot to watch Illuminations with a late dinner reservation.

Restaurant: San Angel Inn
Location: Mexico Pavilion
Meals Available: Lunch and Dinner
Cost: Adults $$, Kids $, Disney Dining Plan: one table-service credit per person

Come inside the Aztec pyramid in the Mexico Pavilion and enjoy a water-side table as guests on the Gran Fiesta Tour go sailing by, or get a table near the "open-air" shopping area. The food is inspired by the actual San Angel Inn in Mexico.

Restaurant: Spice Road Table
Location: Morocco Pavilion
Meals Available: Lunch and Dinner

Cost: Adults $$, Kids $, Disney Dining Plan: one table-service credit per person

You can sit inside or in the large seating area outside along the World Showcase Lagoon. There are extensive "small plate" and entrée menus featuring chicken, lamb, and seafood dishes. This is a great restaurant to get a late reservation and watch Illuminations from the open-air seating area.

Restaurant: Teppan Edo
Location: Japan Pavilion
Meals Available: Lunch and Dinner
Cost: Adults $$, Kids $, Disney Dining Plan: one table-service credit per person

Watch your food get made right in front you at Teppan Edo. This Japanese restaurant specializes in teppanyaki-style cooking with beef, chicken, and seafood dishes cooked and presented right at your table. A fun meal for the entire family.

At Teppan Edo, you'll watch the chef prepare your meal as part of an entertaining show, and their shrimp is delicious. There will be three different dipping sauces. The ranch is my favorite.
— Christina Matt, 9

Restaurant: Tokyo Dining
Location: Japan Pavilion
Meals Available: Lunch and Dinner
Cost: Adults $$, Kids $, Disney Dining Plan: one table-service credit per person

For those guests looking for a more traditional Japanese meal, head on over to Tokyo Dining for some of the finest sushi at Disney World. The meals are served on either traditional plates or in bento boxes.

Restaurant: Tutto Italia
Location: Italy Pavilion

Meals Available: Lunch and Dinner
Cost: Adults $$, Kids $, Disney Dining Plan: one table-service credit per person

Tutto Italia is the intimate dining experience of the two Italian restaurants in Epcot. You're treated to fine Italian cuisine. This restaurant features the "heavier" Italian dishes: filling pastas and lasagnas, pan-fried steaks and fish, and rich desserts.

Restaurant: Via Napoli
Location: Italy Pavilion
Meals Available: Lunch and Dinner
Cost: Adults $$, Kids $, Disney Dining Plan: one table-service credit per person

Via Napoli is the direct opposite of Tutto Italia. It's the "noisy neighbor", with family-style long table seating, but seating for just a single family as well. High ceilings help keep the noise level down. The food is "lighter" than at Tutto Italia. Via Napoli has the best pizza in Disney World.

Restaurant: Biergarten
Location: Germany Pavilion
Meals Available: Lunch and Dinner
Cost: Adults $$, Kids $, Disney Dining Plan: one table-service credit per person

Modeled after a German biergarten, this restaurant features family-style seating at long tables with the food served at a buffet. In the background, German bands entertain; dancing is permitted and encouraged.

> *I really liked the variety of foods they had on the buffet. The music and entertainment were awesome. We laughed and danced all through lunch.*
> — Olivia Nicely, 10

Hollywood Studios

Restaurant: 50s Prime Time Cafe
Location: Echo Lake
Meals Available: Lunch and Dinner
Cost: Adults $$, Kids $, Disney Dining Plan: one table-service credit per person

Head back in time to your grandparents' kitchen when they were kids and enjoy a meal at the 50s Prime Time Café. The décor of the restaurant is a 1950s kitchen with thin-legged chairs and tiny televisions showing programs from the era. Be nice to your server and make sure you are a member of the "clean plate club" so you can get dessert.

My favorite restaurant is the 50s Prime Time Cafe because of the atmosphere. I love how the waiters and waitresses stay in character and treat you like family.
— Nia Donfris, 14

Restaurant: Hollywood Brown Derby
Location: Hollywood Boulevard
Meals Available: Lunch and Dinner
Cost: Adults $$$, Kids $, Disney Dining Plan: two table-service credits per person

The finest dining in Hollywood Studios, the Brown Derby brings you back to the early 20th century and the Golden Age of Hollywood. The restaurant is known for its famous Cobb Salad served at lunch and dinner.

Restaurant: Mama Melrose
Location: Streets of America
Meals Available: Lunch and Dinner
Cost: Adults $$, Kids $, Disney Dining Plan: one table-service credit per person

Mama Melrose serves Italian food with an American flair like "mama" used to make back home. The focus is more on the "filling/heavier" Italian dishes, so you rarely leave hungry. Good food at a good price at Hollywood Studios.

Restaurant: Sci-Fi Dine-In
Location: Commissary Lane
Meals Available: Lunch and Dinner
Cost: Adults $$, Kids $, Disney Dining Plan: one table-service credit per person

One of the best themed restaurants at Hollywood Studios, You sit at a table designed like a car from the 50s and 60s while you watch science fiction trailers on the big screen. The food served here is traditional all-American fare.

You can eat a meal while sitting in a car at the Sci-Fi Dine-In while watching fun drive-in movie shorts.

— Ben Bratton, 12

Magic Kingdom

Restaurant: Be Our Guest
Location: Fantasyland
Meals Available: Breakfast, Lunch, and Dinner
Cost: Adults $$$, Kids $, Disney Dining Plan: one table-service credit per person

Be Our Guest is located in the Beast's Castle in the new section of Fantasyland. The restaurant is a quick-service credit for breakfast and lunch, and a table-service credit for dinner. Seating for all three meals is reservation only. At lunch, you can select your meal before you even arrive in Disney World or you can choose it when you get there. One of the best lunch items is the braised pork platter.

Restaurant: Liberty Tree Tavern
Location: Liberty Square
Meals Available: Lunch and Dinner
Cost: Adults $$, Kids $, Disney Dining Plan: one table-service credit per person

Liberty Tree Tavern takes guests back to the Colonial era for a great meal with different serving styles for lunch and dinner. Lunch is a traditional a la carte (choose off a menu) style of ordering, while dinner is a family-style meal with a large plate filled with turkey, roast beef, and roast pork along with all the vegetables you can eat—but don't worry if you run out of anything, as they will bring more. An interesting fact about Liberty Tree Tavern is that none of the restrooms are located in Liberty Square. That is because public restrooms did not exist in Colonial times. The restrooms for the Liberty Tree Tavern are located within the restaurant building but in Frontierland and Fantasyland, respectivefully.

Restaurant: Plaza Restaurant
Location: Main Street USA
Meals Available: Lunch and Dinner
Cost: Adults $$, Kids $, Disney Dining Plan: one table-service credit per person

Located at the far end of Main Street and close to Cinderella Castle, Plaza Restaurant is one of the best dining values in the Magic Kingdom. The menu is nothing flashy; just good, solid sandwiches and entrees to fill you up for a day in the parks. Plus, the restaurant has access to the entire Plaza Ice Cream Parlor menu for dessert.

Restaurant: Tony's Town Square
Location: Main Street USA
Meals Available: Lunch and Dinner
Cost: Adults $$, Kids $, Disney Dining Plan: one table-service credit per person

Inspired by the Italian restaurant from *Lady and the Tramp*, Tony's brings Italian cuisine with an American flair to the Magic Kingdom. It's one of the first things you see when you enter the park. It's a great value and a wonderful place to watch people enter and exit the Magic Kingdom.

Disney Springs

Restaurant: Fulton's Crab House
Location: Marketplace
Meals Available: Dinner Only
Cost: Adults $$$, Kids $, Disney Dining Plan: two table-service credits per person

One of the top seafood restaurants in Disney World, Fulton's Crab House brings seafood specialties from around the United States to one location. Plenty of beef and chicken entrées dot the menu as well.

Restaurant: Planet Hollywood
Location: West Side
Meals Available: Lunch and Dinner
Cost: Adults $$, Kids $, Disney Dining Plan: one table-service credit per person

Movie stars from around the world have donated their film memorabilia to Planet Hollywood to create a unique dining experience. Food is all-American fare.

Restaurant: Portobello Country Italian Trattoria
Location: The Landing
Meals Available: Lunch and Dinner
Cost: Adults $$$, Kids $, Disney Dining Plan: one table-service credit per person

Fine Italian dining comes to Disney Springs at Portobello Country Italian Trattoria. As you have noticed, I divide Italian food into "light" and "heavy" dishes. Portobello gives you both with a menu that rotates frequently to give you a true taste of Italy in Florida.

Restaurant: Raglan Road
Location: The Landing
Meals Available: Lunch and Dinner
Cost: Adults $$, Kids $, Disney Dining Plan: one table-service credit per person

Raglan Road brings a party atmosphere to Disney Springs with Irish bands and Irish dancing going on during your meal. The menu is very diverse with both American and Irish dishes You will have a fun time dining at Raglan Road.

Raglan Road in Downtown Disney is my favorite restaurant, it has the best music and dancers.
— Hayden Micun, 10

Restaurant: The BOATHOUSE
Location: The Landing
Meals Available: Dinner Only
Cost: Adults $$$$, Kids $$, Not on Disney Dining Plan

One of the newest restaurants in Disney Springs, the BOATHOUSE offers high-end/very expensive beef and seafood. You can enjoy plenty of water-side seating and even a ride in an aquacar (for an additional fee) before or after your meal.

Restaurant: Wolfgang Puck Grand Cafe
Location: West Side
Meals Available: Lunch and Dinner
Cost: Adults $$$$, Kids $$, Disney Dining Plan: two table-service credits per person

Wolfgang Puck lends his name to one of the finest dining establishments at Disney Springs. The restaurant blends both Asian and California cuisine into a series of spectacular entrees which will please both the foodie and non-foodie in your traveling party.

Non-Character Meals at the Resorts

Restaurant: Artist Point
Location: Wilderness Lodge
Meals Available: Dinner Only

Cost: Adults $$$$, Kids $$, Disney Dining Plan: two table-service credits per person

Luxury dining with a Pacific-Northwest flair, Artist Point brings the fine cuisine of that region to your table. Plenty of seafood and beef dishes are found on the menu.

Restaurant: Beaches and Cream
Location: Beach Club
Meals Available: Lunch and Dinner
Cost: Adults $$, Kids $, Disney Dining Plan: one table-service credit per person

Visit a 50s-era soda shop at Beaches and Cream. This restaurant has standard fare like hamburgers and hot dogs. The restaurant is known for its ice cream specialties like the Kitchen Sink—a dessert big enough to feed the whole family.

Restaurant: Big River Grill
Location: BoardWalk
Meals Available: Lunch and Dinner
Cost: Adults $$$, Kids $, Not a member of the Disney Dining Plan

A brew pub on Disney's BoardWalk, this restaurant serves food much like you will find at the brew pubs back home, with reasonable prices. Another plus is the proximity to the family activities on the BoardWalk. Big River Grill is not on the Disney Dining Plan and, from my experience, does not take advanced dining reservations.

Restaurant: Boatwright's Dining Hall
Location: Port Orleans Riverside
Meals Available: Dinner Only
Cost: Adults $$$, Kids $, Disney Dining Plan: one table-service credit per person

Boatwright's Dining Hall provides guests staying or visiting Port Orleans Riverside a quiet place to grab some dinner after a day in the parks. Boatwright's serves a surf-and-turf menu with emphasis on the surf. Another restaurant where it is easy to get a reservation on short notice.

Restaurant: Boma—Flavors of Africa
Location: Animal Kingdom
Meals Available: Breakfast and Dinner
Cost: Adults $$$$, Kids $$, Disney Dining Plan: one table-service credit per person

Open for breakfast and dinner, Boma is an all-you-can-eat buffet inside Animal Kingdom Lodge. Breakfast is an American-style breakfast buffet with an African flair. At dinner, you'll find both African style and American cuisine served in a great location to end your day in the parks.

> *Boma offers a great selection of African food but also has "safety foods" everyone will like. For drinks, Boma has paper straws which are animal friendly.*
> — Ben Bratton, 12

Restaurant: California Grill
Location: Contemporary Resort
Meals Available: Dinner Only
Cost: Adults $$$$, Kids $$, Disney Dining Plan: two table-service credits per person

With luxury dining on the 15th floor of the Contemporary, this is an ideal location to watch the fireworks over the Magic Kingdom. It's only open for dinner. You'll find expansive sushi selections to go along with the rest of its traditionally California menu.

Restaurant: Captain's Grille
Location: Yacht Club
Meals Available: Breakfast, Lunch, and Dinner
Cost: Adults $$$, Kids $, Disney Dining Plan: one table-service credit per person

Open for breakfast, lunch, and dinner, guests eating at Captain's Grille will find quality food at a value price compared to other restaurants inside Disney's deluxe resorts. This is a great place to start your park day, take a mid-day breaks, or enjoy a nice meal at the end of the day.

Restaurant: Citricos
Location: Grand Floridian
Meals Available: Dinner Only
Cost: Adults $$$$, Kids $$, Disney Dining Plan: two table-service credits per person

A taste of Italy inside the Grand Floridian, Citricos brings you fine Italian-style dining. The menu isn't full pasta, but includes hearty entrees like beef, chicken, pork, and fish.

Restaurant: ESPN Club
Location: BoardWalk
Meals Available: Lunch and Dinner
Cost: Adults $$, Kids $, Not on the Disney Dining Plan

It's game on at the ESPN Club along Disney's BoardWalk. This restaurant is a great place to catch a game with some friends or just get caught in the real-life sports world, just a short walk from Epcot. You'll find well-priced food and entertainment options for everyone.

Restaurant: Flying Fish
Location: BoardWalk
Meals Available: Dinner Only
Cost: Adults $$$, Kids $$, Disney Dining Plan: two table-service credits per person

One of the best seafood restaurants at Disney World,. Flying Fish is the highlight of the BoardWalk. Don't let the name deceive you—there is plenty of beef and pasta on the menu as well.

Restaurant: Grand Floridian Café
Location: Grand Floridian
Meals Available: Breakfast, Lunch, and Dinner
Cost: Adults $$, Kids $, Disney Dining Plan: one table-service credit per person

A great place to get away from the hustle and bustle of the parks, the Grand Floridian Café provides excellent value in one of Disney's finest resorts. The Grand Sandwich, usually served at lunch, is the restaurant's specialty. Just a short boat ride from Magic Kingdom.

Restaurant: Jiko—The Cooking Place
Location: Animal Kingdom
Meals Available: Dinner Only
Cost: Adults $$$$, Kids $$, Disney Dining Plan: two table-service credits per person

Serving African-style cuisine featuring food cooked in two wood-fired ovens, Jiko is a great location inside Animal Kingdom Lodge with some of the best dishes at a resort restaurant. After dinner, youan wander the lodge and look for animals roaming on the savannah. Attire for Jiko is resort-causal (no tank-tops or cut-off shorts permitted).

Restaurant: Kona Cafe
Location: Polynesian Village
Meals Available: Breakfast, Lunch, and Dinner
Cost: Adults $$, Kids $, Disney Dining Plan: one table-service credit per person

Kona Café serves food with a Polynesian flair in a wonderful location inside the Polynesian. The marquee item is the Tonga Toast served at breakfast. Guests enjoying lunch or dinner at Kona Café will find traditional food with Polynesian touches along with an extensive sushi menu.

Restaurant: Maya Grille
Location: Coronado Springs
Meals Available: Dinner Only
Cost: Adults $$, Kids $, Disney Dining Plan: one table-service credit per person

Mexican cuisine meets the American Southwest at the Maya Grille. Plenty of Mexican dishes dot the menu at this restaurant inside Coronado Springs. Maya Grille is only open for dinner and, at times, a one-man mariachi band will play selections from Mexico as well as popular music from the 60s, 70s, and 80s.

Restaurant: Narcoossee's
Location: Grand Floridian
Meals Available: Dinner Only
Cost: Adults $$$$, Kids $$, Disney Dining Plan: two table-service credits per person

One of the finer dining establishments at Disney World, Narcoossee's is only open at dinner time. You have views of the Seven Seas Lagoon along with the Electrical Water Pageant and the Wishes fireworks show from Magic Kingdom. The menu is surf-and-turf. Attire for is resort-causal (no tank-top and cut-off shorts).

Restaurant: Olivia's Cafe
Location: Old Key West
Meals Available: Breakfast, Lunch, and Dinner
Cost: Adults $$, Kids $, Disney Dining Plan: one table-service credit per person

If you're looking for a good value at Disney's original DVC resort, head out to Old Key West to Olivia's. This restaurant is open for breakfast, lunch, and dinner, and serves traditional American cuisine with a Southern flair. Large portions for a good price.

Restaurant: Sanaa
Location: Animal Kingdom
Meals Available: Lunch and Dinner
Cost: Adults $$, Kids $, Disney Dining Plan: one table-service credit per person

Look out over the savannah while enjoying a four-course meal which starts with Sanaa's signature Indian bread service. One of the best values at Disney World and the only restaurant which overlooks the savannah. Other courses feature food inspired by the cuisines of East Africa.

Restaurant: Shutters
Location: Caribbean Beach
Meals Available: Dinner Only
Cost: Adults $$, Kids $, Disney Dining Plan: one table-service credit per person

The cuisine of the Caribbean comes to life at Shutter's inside the Caribbean Beach. This restaurant, like the Maya Grille, is only open for dinner. There is something for everyone's palate at Shutters.

Restaurant: Trail's End
Location: Fort Wilderness
Meals Available: Breakfast, Lunch, and Dinner
Cost: Adults $$, Kids $, Disney Dining Plan: one table-service credit per person

Enjoy food in an Old West American setting at Trail's End. Guests can start the day with one of the most affordable meals on Disney property in the Bounty Breakfast which costs under nine dollars. Lunch is an la carte menu while dinner is a buffet.

Restaurant: Trattoria al Forno
Location: Boardwalk
Meals Available: Breakfast and Dinner
Cost: Adults $$, Kids $, Disney Dining Plan: one table-service credit per person

The newest restaurant along Disney's BoardWalk, Trattoria al Forno adds another Italian restaurant to the Disney World lineup. The menu takes guests on a tour of Italy with lots of pasta and meat dishes. The breakfast menu features a traditional American-style breakfast items.

Restaurant: Turf Club
Location: Saratoga Springs
Meals Available: Dinner Only
Cost: Adults $$, Kids $, Disney Dining Plan: one table-service credit per person

Step into the clubhouse at the Turf Club in Saratoga Springs for a traditionally American menu. After the meal, you can tour the Lake Buena Vista Golf Course clubhouse and see the memorabilia from horse racing venues around the United States.

Restaurant: Victoria and Albert's
Location: Grand Floridian
Meals Available: Dinner Only
Cost: Adults $$$$, Kids $$$, Not on the Disney Dining Plan

The finest dining at Disney World. You'll enjoy cuisine prepared by some of the best chefs from around world. Attire is suit jackets for men and boys, and dresses, pant suits, or long skirts for women and girls.

Restaurant: Wave of American Flavors
Location: Contemporary
Meals Available: Breakfast, Lunch, and Dinner
Cost: Adults $$, Kids $, Disney Dining Plan: one table-service credit per person

Dining in a relaxed atmosphere on the first floor of the Contemporary. As the name suggests, cuisine from around the United States is available here. This restaurant is a great place to start or end the day in the parks, since it is within walking distance from Magic Kingdom.

Restaurant: Whispering Canyon
Location: Wilderness Lodge
Meals Available: Breakfast, Lunch, and Dinner
Cost: Adults $$, Kids $, Disney Dining Plan: one table-service credit per person

Stop in for some of the best interactions with your server at Disney World. The food is a great as well, and good value for the money. A great location to have a large family dinner. Be sure to ask your server for ketchup and plenty of refills on drinks.

Restaurant: Yachtsman Steakhouse
Location: Yacht Club
Meals Available: Dinner Only
Cost: Adults $$$, Kids $, Disney Dining Plan: two table-service credits per person

One of the best steakhouses on Disney World property, the Yachtsman is within walking distance to Epcot and Hollywood Studios. It's a wonderful place to end the day in the parks and maybe take a post-dinner walk to catch Illuminations at Epcot or the fireworks show at Hollywood Studios.

CHAPTER TEN

Value Resorts

All-Star Movies

All Star Movies has 10 buildings with 1920 hotel rooms grouped into five "pods". 101 Dalmatians, Fantasia, and Toy Story are the three pods closest to the main Cinema Hall which houses the food court. The Mighty Ducks and Love Bug pods have a further walk to Cinema Hall.

In terms of space, the rooms at the All-Star Resorts and Pop Century are the smallest on Disney property at only 260 square feet, putting them on par with a standard hotel room at a national chain. The rooms sleep four people. Five people can stay in a All-Star Movie room provided one of the five is under three years old AND sleeps in a crib.

I know a family who stayed at one of the All-Star resorts recently and had to leave their stroller in the car because with two adults, one child aged 3–9, and another child under two years old with a crib, there simply wasn't enough room for everything and everyone.

Even though these are the smallest rooms on Disney property, they are also the least expensive on Disney property. Rack rates run as low, depending on the season, as $90/nt during the week and $110/nt on the weekend.

Guests check in at the Cinema Hall which also houses the food court for the resort. The food court has five different stations (marquee venues) for you to choose from.

There are two pools: the Fantasia Pool which is located centrally between Cinema Hall and the Fantasia pod and features a kids area. The Duck Pond Pool is in the Mighty Ducks pod of the resort.

All-Star Music

All-Star Music is slightly smaller than All-Star Movies with only 1604 rooms, but still large compared to other resorts. The set-up is similar to All-Star Movies: 10 buildings broken up into five pods. The Calypso Pod is closest to the main building, Melody Hall, followed (in terms of distance) by the Jazz Inn, Rock Inn, Broadway Hotel, and Country Fair.

The rooms are music-themed and are 260 square feet, just like at All-Star Movies, with two double beds or one king bed.

There are also family suites available here that at 520 square feet are double the size of a standard room and can sleep up to six people. The suites have one standard queen-sized bed, a queen-sized sofa sleeper, and ottoman/chair sleeper. Each of those can sleep up to two people. The room also has a kitchenette and a fridge and two full-sized bathrooms.

Melody Hall is where guests will check-in and is home to the Intermission Food Court.

Like All-Star Movies, All-Star Music has two pools. The Calypso Pool is located directly in front of Melody Hall and between the two Calypso pod buildings. The Piano Pool is located deeper in the resort and surrounded by the other four pods.

There are two different rack rates for All-Star Music. The Calypso pod is considered the preferred location are costs roughly $15/nt more than the standard locations.

All-Star Sports

The sports-themed All-Star Sports is like All-Star Movies with 1920 rooms, but does not have family suites like at All-Star Music. It does have the familiar 10-building/five-pod set-up. The Surfs Up and Touchdown pods are closest to the main Stadium Hall, while the Center Court, Homerun Hotel, and Hoops Hall are farther away.

The rooms are 260 square feet like the All-Star Movies and Music resorts and can sleep a maximum of five guests.

The Stadium Hall is home to the newly renovated End Zone Food Court.

The resort also has two pools. Surfboard Bay is located directly in front of Stadium Hall and the Grand Slam Pool, complete with Goofy water spout in front of the Home Run Hotel. The kids pool is located at the Surfboard Bay Pool.

Transportation to the parks (by bus, unless otherwise noted) takes approximately:

- Animal Kingdom: 15 minutes
- Epcot: 18 minutes
- Hollywood Studios: 15 minutes
- Magic Kingdom: 18 minutes

Art of Animation

The family suites here opened in May 2012 and the standard rooms in September of that year. The resort has more family suites (1120) than standard rooms (984).

Disney has stuck with the 10-building system for the rooms with a central Animation Hall. Unlike the All-Stars, there are only four pods: Cars, Finding Nemo, the Lion King, and the Little Mermaid. Little Mermaid has standard rooms whereas the other three pods have family suites.

The rooms at Art of Animation are slightly larger than those at the All-Star resorts. Standard rooms are 277 square feet and the family suites are 565 square feet.

Art of Animation has three pools. The central pool is the the Big Blue Pool between the Finding Nemo buildings. The Cars area has its own Cozy Cone Pool, and the Flippin' Fins pool is located by the Little Mermaid buildings.

Animation Hall is where guests check-in. The Landscape of Flavors is the resorts' food court. Like the All-Star resorts, there is no table-service restaurant, just the quick-service food court.

As a relatively new resort, the rack rates are a little higher than the All-Star Resorts.

Transportation to the parks (by bus, unless otherwise noted) takes approximately:

- Animal Kingdom: 20 minutes
- Epcot: 15 minutes
- Hollywood Studios: 15 minutes
- Magic Kingdom: 22 minutes

Pop Century

This resort, the largest at Disney World, has 2880 rooms. Only half of the resort was actually built. The original plan was two main resorts: 1950s through 1990s and 1900s through 1940s. However, only the 50s through 90s section was built. The area that was planned for the 1900s–40s was eventually converted into the Art of Animation.

There are five main pods in the resort. The 50s and the 80s are the largest pods with three buildings, while the 90s pod, at one building, is the smallest.

Rooms are the same size as the rooms at the All-Star resorts—260 square feet—and are themed by decade.

Guests check in at Classic Hall which is also where the Everything Pop food court is located. Like the other value resorts, there is no table-service dining, just the quick-service food court.

Guests have three pools to choose from. The Hippie Dippie Pool is located between the 60s buildings. The

Computer Pool in the 80s and 90s area, and the Bowling Pin Pool is in the 50s area.

Rates for the Pop Century Resort are lower than the Art of Animation, but higher than the All-Star resorts.

Transportation to the parks (by bus, unless otherwise noted) takes approximately:

- Animal Kingdom: 20 minutes
- Epcot: 15 minutes
- Hollywood Studios: 15 minutes
- Magic Kingdom: 22 minutes

CHAPTER ELEVEN

Moderate Resorts

Caribbean Beach Resort

Caribbean Beach is located between Epcot and Hollywood Studios. There are 33 buildings along the 42-acre Barefoot Bay Lake. The buildings are only two-stories high, so you don't have worry about a high-rise building blocking the view from the room. The 33 buildings are connected by a 1.4 mile walking trail.

Everything is centered on the Old Port Royale (also called Centertown): the Market Street Food Court (quick-service dining), Shutters (a table-service restaurant), bicycle and boat rentals, and the pirate-themed main pool.

The resort has nine pools in total. Given its size, this is a necessity because it can be up to a 15-minute walk from Old Port Royale to the outer buildings. Each village (there are six: Trinidad North, Trinidad South, Jamaica, Aruba, Barbados, and Martinique) has its own beach area. Jamaica and Aruba are located on the other side of the lake from the other four villages and Old Port Royale. There is a connector bridge over the lake to get to these two villages. However, there is no swimming in the lake.

Bikes and boats are available for rent at the Barefoot Bay Marina located within Old Port Village. Sea Raycers, sailboats, pontoon boats (up to eight people), canoes, and paddle boats are also available. Motorboats are only rented to guests 12 and over AND at least 5 feet tall. To rent a pontoon boats, you must be 18 and over.

Food is available at the Market Street Food Court, a quick service open from 6 a.m. until midnight. Caribbean Beach also has a table-service restaurant at Shutters.

The rooms at Caribbean Beach are 340 square feet compared to the 260 square feet at the value resorts. Some of the rooms have been converted into pirate-themed rooms.

Transportation to the parks (by bus, unless otherwise noted) takes approximately:

- Animal Kingdom: 23 minutes
- Epcot: 12 minutes
- Hollywood Studios: 12 minutes
- Magic Kingdom: 15 minutes

I love Caribbean Beach because they have two pools-one for the big kids to play in and one for the little kids to play in and it's right by the food court so you can get snacks and drinks too.

— Corbin Wiltse, 11

Coronado Springs Resort

Coronado Springs is located near Animal Kingdom. It's a big resort with buildings around Lago Dorado. The buildings here are only two or three stories high. The front desk and main dining areas are separate. The front desk is located on one side of the convention center while the dining (Pepper Market and Maya Grill) are located on the other.

A stepped Mayan Pyramid frames the 120'x90' Dig Site pool with water slide. There is a playground/archaeological dig site for kids by The Dig Site as well.

The buildings surround Lago Dorado. As a result, some of the buildings are a healthy walk from the front of the resort, convention center, and restaurants. To counter this, Coronado Springs has its own internal shuttle service.

There is no boat rental available at Coronado Springs. There is bike rental.

The quick-service restaurant at Coronado Springs, the Pepper Market, is open from 6 a.m. to 11 p.m. There is also a table-service restaurant, Maya Grill. The Rix Lounge is open until 2 a.m.

The rooms are little smaller than the Caribbean Beach rooms, at 314 square feet, and can accommodate up to four guests.

Transportation to the parks (by bus, unless otherwise noted) takes approximately:

- Animal Kingdom: 20 minutes
- Epcot: 13 minutes
- Hollywood Studios: 13 minutes
- Magic Kingdom: 18 minutes

Port Orleans

Port Orleans is two resorts in one. There are two locations: French Quarter and Riverside. The resort itself is located between Epcot and Disney Springs. This is another massive resort in terms of layout. Each area has its own check-in location. The French Quarter is more "land-locked" than Riverside, where the buildings surround the river.

Each part of the resort has its own main pool. The French Quarter has the Doobloon Lagoon and Riverside has the Ol' Man Island Fishing Hole. There are smaller pools throughout both halves of the resort.

Like Caribbean Beach, there are both bike and boat rentals at Port Orleans. Bikes can be rented from 9 a.m. to 5 p.m. daily, while boats can be rented from 10 a.m. to 5 p.m. daily.

Unlike Caribbean Beach and Coronado Springs, there is no table-service restaurant at French Quarter. There is only the quick-service Sassagoula Floatworks and Food Factory. If you're looking for table-service dining, head over to Riverside and dine at Boatwright's. Riverside has its own quick-service food court at the Riverside Mill.

Rooms at French Quarter can accommodate up to four people. Riverside can accommodate up to five people with the addition of a pull out Murphy bed in some of the rooms. Riverside is the larger of the two resorts, with 2,048 rooms compared to 1,000 rooms at French Quarter.

Transportation to the parks (by bus, unless otherwise noted) takes approximately:

- Animal Kingdom: 26 minutes
- Epcot: 26 minutes
- Hollywood Studios: 14 minutes
- Magic Kingdom: 17 minutes

Yehaa Bob on the piano at the River Roost Lounge at Disney's Port Orleans Resort-Riverside is the best hidden attraction in all of Walt Disney World. Don't forget to tell him his hair looks great!
— Ben Bratton, 12

What I love about Port Orleans French Quarter is going down the serpent slide at the pool, the beautiful rooms, and the beignets at Sassagoula's. At the parade there, they lend out instruments to children who want to participate and pass out beads and gold coins.
— Cecelia Matt, 8

Fort Wilderness Cabins and Campground

Located between Epcot and the Magic Kingdom is the Fort Wilderness Cabins and Campground, one of the original Disney resorts. Given its primary function as a resort for people who come down in RVs and wish to camp on Disney property, it's another big resort with 800 campsites and 409 cabins sprinkled throughout the campground.

Guests check-in at the Reception Outpost. The cabins are 12'x42' and have a sleeping area and living/cooking area. Each cabin has a full bathroom with shower. There are 15 comfort stations throughout the resort with private showers for guests who have come down to camp on property.

Like Coronado Springs, Fort Wilderness has its own internal transportation system. The resort is 1.5 miles long and .5 miles wide.

The resort has two pools. The main pool is located at the center of the resort and a smaller pool is located by the resort's main entrance.

The campgrounds have two restaurants and two dinner shows located on property. Snacks and pizza can be found at Crockett's Tavern. An all-you-can eat buffet at Trails End serves breakfast, lunch and dinner. The two dinner shows are Mickey's Backyard BBQ held on select evenings at the Fort Wilderness Pavilion and the Hoop Dee Doo Musical Revue (two table-service DDP credits each).

Transportation to the parks (by bus, unless otherwise noted) takes approximately:

- Animal Kingdom: 24 minutes
- Epcot: 13 minutes
- Hollywood Studios: 18 minutes
- Magic Kingdom: 16 minutes (boat)

CHAPTER TWELVE

Deluxe Resorts

Animal Kingdom Lodge

Animal Kingdom Lodge is the largest, in terms of rooms, of the deluxe resorts, with 1,307 rooms. All of the Animal Kingdom Lodge rooms are located in the Jambo House.

The front desk and check-in is located in the central main hall with four trails splitting off from this hall. There are four trails where the rooms are located: Ostrich Trail, Giraffe Trail, Kudu Trail, and Zebra Trail. Each of these trails, except for Giraffe, has a view of at least one savanna. Giraffe Trail has a view of the pool.

There are only 135 rooms (10.3%) which do not have a view of a savanna or pool. Sunset Savanna and Sunset Savanna Viewing Room/Balcony are designed for sunset viewing of the animals. Each savanna has a variety of viewing location and cast members will move around the savanna with the animals.

The Sunrise Breakfast Adventure is available on Sundays and Thursdays. It departs at 7:30 a.m. and involves a 45-minute ride through the Kilimanjaro Safari Experience where the guides will stop and guests are allowed to stand and take picture. This ride is about three times as long as the theme park version of Kilimanjaro Safari.. After the tour, you're taken to Pizzafari for a breakfast buffet.

Animal Kingdom Lodge is home to Disney's largest pool, Uzima Springs, at over 11,000 square feet. It has a zero-depth entry section, a 67-foot water slide, and wading area. The pool is open 24 hours, but lifeguards go off duty at 10 p.m.

A standard room at Animal Kingdom Lodge is 344 square feet and can sleep four or five people.

The resort has two table-service restaurants: Jiko, a fusion of American and African cuisine, but open for dinner only, and Boma, a buffet featuring African cuisine, and open for both breakfast and dinner. Quick-service dining is found at Mara and serves traditional American fare for breakfast, lunch, and dinner.

Transportation to the parks (by bus, unless otherwise noted) takes approximately:

- Animal Kingdom: 18 minutes
- Epcot: 20 minutes
- Hollywood Studios: 19 minutes
- Magic Kingdom: 21 minutes

I like Animal Kingdom Lodge because it has a great view of the animals. And they leave little chocolates on your bed.
— Corbin Wiltse, 11

Beach and Yacht Club

The Beach Club is themed after a Newport Beach cottage, while the Yacht Club has a Martha's Vineyard theme and is seen as the more formal of the two. Yacht Club has more standard rooms and also houses the convention center, adding to the more "business-like" feel.

The two resorts also share a central pool area, Stormalong Bay, which has the longest water slide of any Disney resort. The slide goes over the sidewalk and winds its way into the pool area. There are quiet, smaller pool located through both resorts.

The rooms at Beach Club are a large 381 square feet. Two different views are available: standard and pool/water, which will have a view of each the pool or of Crescent Lake.

The resort has two table-service restaurants. Beaches and Cream is a 1950s-style soda shop that serves hamburgers, hot dogs, and the famous Kitchen Sink sundae. There is outdoor seating; the limited indoor seating area can be quite loud. Cape May Cafe is open for breakfast and dinner. The breakfast buffet features is a character meal with Goofy and friends in beach wear. Dinner is a clambake buffet, but plenty of other selections are available. The Beach Club Marketplace is the quick-service dining option.

The resort has two lit tennis-courts which are open from 7 a.m. to 10 p.m., a beach volleyball court, and a health spa.

Beach Club has foot, boat, and bus access to the park. You have the option of walking or taking the boat to both Epcot and Hollywood Studios. You can use the International Gateway entrance to Epcot even when the World Showcase is closed to guests but Future World is open.

Transportation to the parks (by bus, unless otherwise noted) takes approximately:

- Animal Kingdom: 26 minutes
- Epcot: 4 minutes (walk) 22 minutes (boat)
- Hollywood Studios: 25 minutes (walk) 20 minutes (boat)
- Magic Kingdom: 17 minutes

> *I thought I would like the Beach Club, but I found it was too noisy. The best thing here is I felt safe and could walk to Epcot by myself.*
> — Julia Abrams, 16

The Yacht Club has rooms the same size as those of the Beach Club, at 381 square feet. Standard and pool/water view rooms available.

Yacht Club has two table-service restaurants: Yachtsman Steakhouse and Captain's Grille. The Yachtsman Steakhouse is a two table-service credit dinner and one of the best restaurants in Disney World. It serves dinner only.

Right next door is the Captain's Grille, serving breakfast, lunch, and dinner, for one table-service credit. The menu is similar to Yachtsman, but with a little more seafood on the menu.

Yacht Club shares most of its recreational facilities with Beach Club.

Transportation to the parks (by bus, unless otherwise noted) takes approximately:

- Animal Kingdom: 28 minutes
- Epcot: 6 minutes (walk) 22 minutes (boat)
- Hollywood Studios: 20 minutes (boat) 23 minutes (walk)
- Magic Kingdom: 19 minutes

Boardwalk Resort

Across Crescent Lake from Beach and Yacht Club sits the Boardwalk Resort in its early 20th century Atlantic City theme. The resort has both standard rooms and villa style accommodations. My family has stayed in the villas as DVC members, but not in the standard rooms.

The resort has a central check-in for guests of both Boardwalk Inn and Boardwalk Villa. The unique feature of this resort is that none of its restaurants (table or quick service) are located in the resort itself. They are all located along the BoardWalk facing Crescent Lake.

The rooms at Boardwalk are 370 square feet and continue with the early 20th century boardwalk theme.

The resort has one centrally located pool, Luna Park, with its clowns-mouth water slide, or as some people call it, the Scary Clown Pool. There is a quiet pool located in each of the Inn and Villa areas.

There are a lot of restaurants to choose from on the BoardWalk. Some of the restaurants take the Disney Dining Plan and some of them do not. First the ones that do:

Flying Fish Cafe is primarily a seafood restaurant that does have a steak option. It is a two table-credit meal, but it is worth those two credits. My family ate here with another family on our last visit and had an excellent experience. Trattoria al Forno is the other dining plan table-service location on the BoardWalk.

Quick service is covered by two places: the Boardwalk Bakery with its fresh baked breakfast foods and sandwiches for lunch, and the Pizza Window. Seashore Sweets offers snacks.

There are two non-Disney Dining Plan establishments on the BoardWalk: The ESPN Club is a good place to catch a game and a bite to eat, and the Big River Grille and Brewing Works is a micro brewery.

Transportation to the parks (by bus, unless otherwise noted) takes approximately:

- Animal Kingdom: 23 minutes
- Epcot: 8 minutes (walk) 15 minutes (boat)
- Hollywood Studios: 25 minutes (boat or walk)
- Magic Kingdom: 14 minutes

Contemporary Resort

The Contemporary has the unique feature of the monorail going directly through the main concourse of the hotel. There are two types of rooms: tower rooms and garden wing. The standard rooms are large at 391 square feet. There is enough space for three people and their luggage.

You can also view the nightly Magic Kingdom fireworks and the Electric Water Pageant from the balcony of the Grand Canyon Concourse. Guests staying on the 14th floor of the main tower have their own private balcony to watch the fireworks. Guests dining at the 15th floor California Grill Lounge have a private view area as well.

Guests have three table-service restaurants to choose from at the Contemporary. The California Grill serves dinner only and focuses on California-themed cuisine. Serving breakfast, lunch, and dinner, The Wave has a rotating menu of American cuisine. The last restaurant, popular among the young and young at heart, is Chef Mickey's, a buffet where guests meet Mickey and the gang in chef's attire.

The Contemporary has one quick-service restaurant: Contempo Cafe. This is one of my family's favorite quick-service restaurants on property. We enjoy taking in a relaxed meal while watching the people and monorail go by. It has a very "Grand Central Station" feel to it with all the people coming and going.

Guests at the Contemporary have a variety of transportation to get to the parks. The monorail provides access to both Magic Kingdom and Epcot. A transfer is required at the Ticket and Transportation Center to get to Epcot by monorail. You can also walk to Magic Kingdom.

Transportation to the parks (by bus, unless otherwise noted) takes approximately:

- Animal Kingdom: 25 minutes
- Epcot: 34 minutes (monorail includes transfer to Epcot monorail)
- Hollywood Studios: 19 minutes
- Magic Kingdom: 10 minutes (walk) 19 minutes (monorail)

> *A resort for first time people should be the*
> *Contemporary because it has a restaurant in*
> *it and you can see the Magic Kingdom.*
> — Carter Wiltse, 9

Grand Floridian Resort

The Grand Floridian Resort has a Victorian seaside resort theme. It is the closest resort, in terms of monorail stops, to the Magic Kingdom, but does not have direct walking access.

One of the best things about the Grand Floridian is the lobby. It has one of the best themed lobbies on property. The rooms are spectacular, too. They are some of Disney's largest standard rooms, at 440 square feet.

Like most of the deluxe resorts, the Grand Floridian has a central main pool with smaller quiet pools throughout the resort.

The other great feature about the Grand Floridian is the five table-service restaurants located within the resort.

Victoria and Albert's is not on the Disney Dining Plan and a jacket is required for men. The menu is selected daily by the head chef. Citricos features cuisine from southern France and is also open only for dinner. It is resort causal (no jacket required). Located toward the back of the Grand Floridian property is Narcoossee's which serves more traditional American fare. 1900 Park Fare is a character buffet (breakfast and dinner). Breakfast has Mary Poppins and friends, while dinner has the Fairy Godmother, Prince Charming, Cinderella, and the Evil Step Sisters. The most causal of the dining experiences is the Grand Floridian Café, which is open for breakfast, lunch, and dinner. Quick service is available from the 24-hour Gasparilla Island Grill.

Transportation to the parks (by bus, unless otherwise noted) takes approximately:

- Animal Kingdom: 24 minutes
- Epcot: 42 minutes (monorail includes transfer time to Epcot monorail)
- Hollywood Studios: 18 minutes
- Magic Kingdom: 10 minutes (monorail) 17 minutes (boat)

I love The Grand Floridian. I love the
Victorian style and walking through it.
— Nia Donfris, 14

Polynesian Resort

The Polynesian is broken up into long-houses for the rooms. The rooms are smaller than those at the Grand Floridian, but larger than the Contemporary, at 415 square feet.

The resort has two table-service dining options. 'Ohana which serves a family-style breakfast and dinner. Breakfast is a character buffet with Lilo, Stitch, and rotating cast of characters. Kona Cafe serves breakfast, lunch, and dinner, and focuses on American and Asian cuisine. Quick service is located at Captain Cook's, which is open 24 hours.

You have the choice of monorail or boat access to Magic Kingdom. You can also take a short walk to the Ticket and Transportation Center for monorail access to Epcot, and there are bus stops at the Polynesian for Animal Kingdom and Hollywood Studios.

Transportation to the parks (by bus, unless otherwise noted) takes approximately:

- Animal Kingdom: 26 minutes
- Epcot: 39 minutes (monorail including walking time to the Ticket and Transportation Center)
- Hollywood Studios: 20 minutes
- Magic Kingdom: 12 minutes (boat) 13 minutes (monorail)

Wilderness Lodge

Over by Fort Wilderness is the last deluxe resort, Wilderness Lodge, a fantastically theme Pacific Northwest resort. My family and I have stayed here twice: once as resort guests and once as DVC members.

It is a compact resort with the DVC villas in their own wing. The trade-off is the smallest rooms of all the Disney deluxe resorts. Standard rooms are only 340 square feet.

The resort has a central pool shared by both lodge and villa guests, while the villa area has its own quiet pool.

The focal point of the resort is the lobby and its wonderful theming, especially at Christmas time.

The resort has two table-service restaurants. Artist Point is a two table-credit restaurant that serves cuisine with a Pacific Northwest flare. Whispering Canyon Cafe is a one-credit table-service restaurant that has both family style and individual dining options. Be sure to hold onto your fork and to ask your server for more ketchup. Quick-service is located at Roaring Forks. It serves breakfast, lunch, and dinner, but is open only from 7 a.m. to 11 p.m.

You can take the red-flagged boat to Magic Kingdom. The other boat (usually blue flagged) will take guests to Fort Wilderness and the Contemporary.

Wilderness Lodge is the least expensive of the deluxe resorts.

Transportation to the parks (by bus, unless otherwise noted) takes approximately:

- Animal Kingdom: 29 minutes
- Epcot: 22 minutes
- Hollywood Studios: 23 minutes
- Magic Kingdom: 13 minutes (boat)

Check with the front desk at the Wilderness Lodge for a fun Hidden Mickey scavenger hunt throughout the resort.
— Ben Bratton, 12

CHAPTER THIRTEEN

Deluxe Villas

All of the Disney deluxe resorts have deluxe villa accommodations with the exception of the Yacht Club. There are also two resorts which only have villa accommodations: Old Key West and Saratoga Springs.

Most people will refer to these accommodations as DVC, since most guests who stay here are DVC members. DVC is Disney's time-share program where people buy points for their "home resort" which they receive every year until their contract expires. Members use those points to make room reservations, and aren't locked into certain weeks of the year, every year, until their contract expires. Villas come in four sizes: studio, one-bedroom, two-bedroom, and three bedroom grand villas.

Non-members can make reservations at these resorts as well. There is a small percentage of villas which are available for "cash only" reservations, but the cost per night isn't cheap, especially when you get into the two and three bedroom villas. So, if you want to stay in a villa, be prepared to spend big.

All of the studio villas come with a kitchenette. All of the one, two, and grand villa come with a full kitchen (plates, glasses, and cooking utensils provided) and a stacked washer and dryer combo.

Animal Kingdom Villas

Animal Kingdom has two locations for its villas. There are some in the Jambo House with the standard rooms, but most are in Kidani Village. A large portion of the rooms will have a view of the savanna, though some will a view of a pool or of a parking lot. Look kids....OUR CAR!

The studio rooms in Jambo House vary from 316 to 365 square feet while the Kidani Village studios are a standard 366 square feet. These studios sleep four and have a queen-sized bed with full-sized sofa sleeper.

Jambo House has some value villas which will only sleep four guests and vary from 629 to 710 square feet. The Kidani Village one-bedroom villas are 819 square feet. The master bedroom has a king-sized bed. The living area has a dining table, a queen-sized sofa bed, and a twin-sized sleeper chair. The kitchen has a full-sized fridge, stove, microwave, dishwasher, and settings for 8 or 9 people.

The two bedrooms are 1,152 square feet at both Jambo and Kidani. The master bedroom has a king-sized bed with a queen-sized bed in the second bedroom. The living area has a queen-sized sofa bed and twin-sized convertible chair. The kitchen and settings are the same as in the one-bedroom, with settings for 8 or 9 people. There's a bathroom in the master bedroom, and one in the second bedroom.

The grand villas are 2,349 square feet at Jambo House and only one story, while there are slightly smaller (2,201 square feet) grand villas at Kidani Village. However, these villas are two stories. The villas have three bedrooms, three balconies, and a living area in the middle. The master bedroom has a king-sized bed with two queen-sized beds in each of the other bedrooms; there's still a queen-size sofa bed and twin-sized chair sleeper in the living area. The villa comes with two full bathrooms and a dining area which can seat 10 and a bar area which can seat three and comes with dishware for 12–13 guests.

Transportation to the parks (by bus, unless otherwise noted) takes approximately:

- Animal Kingdom: 18 minutes
- Epcot: 20 minutes
- Hollywood Studios: 19 minutes
- Magic Kingdom: 21 minutes

Bay Lake Tower at the Contemporary Resort

I am a DVC member and my home resort is Bay Lake Tower. We chose it because of the ability to walk to Magic Kingdom and monorail access to Epcot: two of our favorite parks. This is also one of DVC's newest properties.

Bay Lake Tower also has the Top of the World Lounge where you can view the Wishes firework show every night. This lounge is, currently, open to all guests staying at a DVC property. Bay Lake Tower has its own lobby area separate from the Contemporary.

Studios at Bay Lake Tower can sleep up to four guests and are 339 square feet. They are the smallest studios within DVC. However, the one bedrooms at Bay Lake Tower are some of the largest, at 801 square feet. These villas can sleep five people. The sofa sleepers in these villas are very comfortable. Unlike most sofa sleepers, you do not feel the springs supporting the sleeper bed.

The master bedroom has a king-sized bed and master bathroom. The living area has a full kitchen, queen-sized sofa sleeper, and a twin-sized convertible chair. These one-bedroom villas also have a full second bathroom for guests. There is also a dining table for 6 or 7 guests and dishware for 8 or 9 guests.

The 1,152 square foot two-bedroom villa can sleep up to nine guests. There is a king-sized bed in the master bedroom and a queen-sized bed and queen-sized sofa bed in the second bedroom with the sofa and chair sleepers in the living area. The dining area has a table for 6 or 7 guests with a bar area for extra seating. There are also two full-sized bathrooms in the two-bedroom villas.

All of the grand villas at Bay Lake Tower are two floors and 2,044 square feet. They can accommodate up to 13 guests. There are two bedrooms on the second floor each with a private bathroom and a living area with a sleeper chair. Downstairs is another bedroom along with a second living area and kitchen/dining area. The dining area has seating for 10 with a bar area for additional seating.

Bay Lake Tower shares bus and monorail stops with the Contemporary.

Transportation to the parks (by bus, unless otherwise noted) takes approximately:

- Animal Kingdom: 25 minutes
- Epcot: 34 minutes (monorail includes transfer to Epcot monorail)
- Hollywood Studios: 19 minutes
- Magic Kingdom: 10 minutes (walk) 19 minutes (monorail)

Beach Club Villas

The Beach Club is slightly different from all the other DVC properties in that there are no grand villas here.

The studios at Beach Club are 365 square feet and sleep up to four guests. They come with a queen-sized bed and a full-sized sofa sleeper.

The one-bedroom villas are smaller, at 726 square feet. These villas can sleep up to four guests. The master bedroom has a king-sized bed. The living area has a queen-sized sofa bed. The dining area has seating for 4 or 5 guests with a bar area for extra seating. Unlike the Bay Lake Tower one-bedroom villas, there is only one bathroom in these.

The two bedrooms at Beach Club are 1,083 square feet, so again they are on the smaller side. They have a master bedroom with a king-sized bed and a second bedroom with a queen-sized bed and either a full-sized or queen-sized sofa bed. The living area also has a queen-sized sofa bed and chair sleeper.

Transportation to the parks (by bus, unless otherwise noted) takes approximately:

- Animal Kingdom: 26 minutes
- Epcot: 4 minutes (walk) 22 minutes (boat)
- Hollywood Studios: 25 minutes (walk) 20 minutes (boat)
- Magic Kingdom: 17 minutes

Boardwalk Villas

Located in a separate wing from the Boardwalk Inn are the Boardwalk Villas.

Studios are 359 square feet and have the standard studio queen-sized bed and full-sized sofa sleeper with kitchenette.

The one-bedroom villas are 712 square feet and can sleep up to four guests. There is a king-sized bed in the master bedroom and a queen-sized sofa bed in the living area. Like Beach Club, there is only one full-sized bathroom in these villas.

The two-bedroom villas are 1,072 square feet and can sleep up to eight guests. The master bedroom has a king-sized bed while the second bedroom has a queen-sized bed with a full or queen-sized sofa sleeper. There is an additional queen-sized sofa sleeper in the living area. There is a full-sized bathroom located off of each bed-room. The dining area has seating for 8 or 9 with additional bar seating.

The grand villas are all one floor and 2,142 square feet, withsleeping space for 13 guests. The master bedroom has a king-sized bed, with two queen beds in each of the other bedrooms. There's a bathroom off each of the three bedrooms. The living area has a queen sofa bed and a dining area for 8 guests.

Transportation to the parks (by bus, unless otherwise noted) takes approximately:

- Animal Kingdom: 23 minutes
- Epcot: 8 minutes (walk) 15 minutes (boat)
- Hollywood Studios: 25 minutes (boat or walk)
- Magic Kingdom: 14 minutes

Grand Floridian

The studios are the Grand Floridian are 374 square feet with a queen-sized and a full-sized sofa sleeper.

The one-bedroom is 844 square feet. The master bedroom has a king sized bed with a queen sofa sleeper in the living area. There is also either a chair sleeper or Murphy-style pull-out bed. The one-bedroom villas also only have one bathroom. There is a dining area for 4 or 5 guests.

The two-bedroom/two-bathroom villas are 1,232 square feet. All the villas come with a master bedroom. The configuration of the other beds is either two queen-sized beds with one sofa sleeper or one queen-sized with two sofa sleepers. The dining area can accommodate 6 or 7 guests with extra bar seating available.

The grand villas are all one floor and 2,800 square feet. These villas can sleep up to 12 people in a master bedroom and two bedrooms each with two queen bed. There is an additional queen sofa sleeper. The villa has three bathrooms off of each bedroom and a dining area which can seat 10 guests with extra bar seating.

Transportation to the parks (by bus, unless otherwise noted) takes approximately:

- Animal Kingdom: 24 minutes
- Epcot: 42 minutes (monorail includes transfer time to Epcot monorail)

- Hollywood Studios: 18 minutes
- Magic Kingdom: 10 minutes (monorail) 17 minutes (boat)

Old Key West

The original DVC property, this resort winds its way through one of the Disney World's golf courses and has a large footprint. The resort also has a table-service restaurant, Olivia's, and a quick-service restaurant, Good's Food to Go, which serves breakfast, lunch, and dinner. Old Key West is a stand-alone resort in that it does not share facilities with another Disney resort like the other DVC properties.

As the original DVC property, the villas at Old Key West are some of the largest. The studio is 392 square feet and features two queen-sized beds. No sofa sleeper at Old Key West in the studios.

The one bedrooms are 942 square feet and sleep up to five guests in a king-sized bed in a master bedroom with a queen-sized sofa sleeper and chair sleeper in the living area. The rooms have only one full-sized bathroom and a dining area which can seat up to four guests.

The two bedroom villas are 1,395 square feet and can sleep up to nine guests. There is a master bedroom with a king bed and two queen beds in the second bedroom with a sofa and chair sleepers in the living area. There are bathrooms located off of each bedroom. The dining area has seating for 4 guests.

The grand villas are 2,375 square feet and sleep up to 13 guests. There are three bedrooms with the master bedroom and its king bed and two additional bedrooms, each with two queen beds and a sofa and chair sleepers in the living area. The dining area can seat 8 guests and there are three bathrooms located off the bedrooms.

Transportation to the parks (by bus, unless otherwise noted) takes approximately:

- Animal Kingdom: 20 minutes
- Epcot: 21 minutes
- Hollywood Studios: 16 minutes
- Magic Kingdom: 25 minutes

Saratoga Springs Resort

This is another DVC property that does not share facilities with another Disney resort and has an early 20th century Saratoga Springs theme. Like Old Key West, it is a large property which borders one of the Disney golf courses. It has the most rooms of all the DVC properties, making it easier to get a cash reservation.

The studios go back to the traditional queen-sized bed and full-sized sofa sleeper set up and are 355 square feet.

The one bedroom can sleep up to four guests and are 714 square feet. They have a king bed in the master bedroom and a queen-sized sofa bed in the living area. There is only one full-sized bathroom and the dining area can seat 4 or 5 people.

The two bedroom villas are 1,075 square feet and can sleep eight guests in a master bedroom with king bed and a second bedroom with two queen-sized beds and a queen sofa sleeper in the living area. There are two full-sized bathrooms The dining area can accommodate 4 or 5 guests with additional bar seating..

All of the grand villas are two floors with two bedrooms each with two queen beds on the second floor and a master bedroom with king bed on the main floor. The living area has a queen sized bed in this 2,113 square-foot villa. There are three full bathrooms and the dining area can seat 10 guests with additional bar seating.

Saratoga Springs also has a unique style of villa on its property: the treehouse villa. This is the second time that Disney has opened these treehouse villas to guests. The first time was in the 1980s when they were called the

Village Resort. I stayed here during that time period. In the 1990s, they were reserved for members of the Disney Institute and then reopened to guests in 2003 as part of Saratoga Springs. They are octagonal in shape both inside and outside. They can accommodate 9 guests and are 1,074 square feet. There are 60 treehouse villas and they are roughly 10 feet off the ground. They have three bedrooms, two bathrooms, and an open kitchen.

Transportation to the parks (by bus, unless otherwise noted) takes approximately:

- Animal Kingdom: 20 minutes
- Epcot: 15 minutes
- Hollywood Studios: 13 minutes
- Magic Kingdom: 12 minutes (monorail) 17 minutes (boat)

Saratoga Springs Resort and Spa has a several pools to enjoy, nightly Disney movies are shown at the main pool, and the resort offers boat transportation to Disney Springs.
— Ben Bratton, 12

Wilderness Lodge Villas

The studio rooms are 356 square and have a queen-sized bed with a full-sized sofa sleeper.

The one bedrooms are 727 square feet with a master bedroom featuring a king bed and a living area with a queen sofa sleeper. The dining area can accommodate four guests and there is one full bathroom.

The two bedroom villas can sleep up to eight in 1,083 square foot. The master bedroom has a king bed with two queen beds in the second bedroom with a queen sofa bed in the living area. The dining area has seating for four and extra bar seating. A full bathroom is off of each bedroom.

Transportation to the parks (by bus, unless otherwise noted) takes approximately:

- Animal Kingdom: 29 minutes
- Epcot: 22 minutes
- Hollywood Studios: 23 minutes
- Magic Kingdom: 13 minutes (boat)

As you've seen and read, these villas can be quite expensive when making a cash reservation. However, there are A LOT of DVC members and some of them cannot use all of their points in a given year. Non-members can rent points from a DVC member to reduce some of the cost.

I recommend only using reputable agencies when renting points for a DVC reservation. Don't go through an individual member unless you know that member very well. When you rent points, the member makes and is in control of the reservation, NOT you. They are making the reservation on your behalf, and yes, there have been incidences when members will pocket the money and either not make a reservation or take the vacation themselves or cancel the reservation and not tell you.

Typical pricing is $14 per point. For a week, a studio will cost 120 points, a one-bedroom 180 points, a two-bedroom 260 points, and a grand villa 600+ points. These point values will vary by DVC resort and time of year.

About the Author

Tim Brooks has been visiting Walt Disney World since the late 1970s. Since then, he has made many more trips to the resort both as a child and now with a family of his own. During those trips, he has built up a wealth of knowledge about the attractions and resorts which make up Disney World. Tim has spent the last two years writing a Disney World blog (dadfordisney.com) and the last 18 months working as an independent travel agent specializing in Disney travel with Fairytale Journeys (fairytalejourneysbytimbrooks.com).

Walt Disney World for Teens and Tweens attempts to fill what Tim thinks is an underserved market in the Disney World guidebook world. There are lots of guidebooks for adults and a few guidebooks for preschool and early elementary school aged children, but not very many for tweens and teens. Using his own tween child as inspiration, Tim decided to write this book with that age group in mind.

More Books from Theme Park Press

Theme Park Press publishes dozens of books each year for Disney fans and for general and academic audiences. Here are just a few of our titles. For the complete catalog, including book descriptions and excerpts, please visit:

ThemeParkPress.com

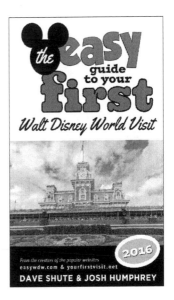

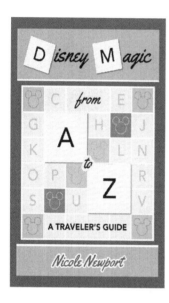

A Historical Tour of
Walt Disney World

ANDREW KISTE

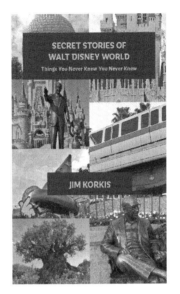

SECRET STORIES OF
WALT DISNEY WORLD
Things You Never Knew You Never Knew

JIM KORKIS

MURDER
IN THE MAGIC KINGDOM

Annie Salisbury

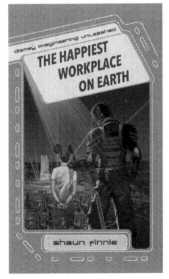

disney imagineering unleashed
THE HAPPIEST
WORKPLACE
ON EARTH

shaun finnie

THE
RIDE DELEGATE
Memoir of a Walt Disney World VIP Tour Guide

Annie Salisbury

The Ultimate
Disney
Vacation Club
Guide

Shaun Brouwer

Epcot's World Showcase
A Pavilion-by-Pavilion Guide

Rick Killingsworth
& Cassie Novak

Would You Like
MAGIC
With That?

WORKING AT
WALT DISNEY WORLD
GUEST RELATIONS

Annie Salisbury

35315620R00095

Made in the USA
Middletown, DE
27 September 2016